CONCISE COLOR GUIDES

Modern Civil Aircraft

General Editor
Derek Avery

W9-BHA-925

Longmeadow Press

This 1988 edition is published by
Longmeadow Press
201 High Ridge Road
Stamford CT 06904

ISBN 0   681   40434   5

Printed in Italy by Amadeus S.p.A. - Rome

0987654

Contents

Introduction

Prior to the First World War there were no scheduled airline services. The postwar 1920s heralded the beginnings of the air transport business, based primarily on cheap conversions of wartime aircraft. Passengers were often exposed to the elements and forced to wear leather coats, gloves, flying helmets and goggles. Passenger comfort soon became a priority, and attempts to provide this forced many of the new unsubsidized airlines either to amalgamate into larger, financially sound operations, or to go out of business. In 1924 the British government amalgamated four struggling airlines to form Imperial Airways, whilst most of their European competitors were already receiving substantial government assistance.

The airlines' second priority was that of speed, and the breakthrough came in 1927, first in the form of the Ryan Broughan, sister ship of Charles Lindbergh's Atlantic-crossing *Spirit of St Louis* and later that same year – the year in which the US Government opened up airmail operations to private enterprise – by the Lockheed Vega.

The airlines remained unprofitable as the faster aircraft were unable to carry heavy loads over long distances and the aircraft capable of doing so were sluggishly slow. The breakthrough here came in 1933 with the development of the twin-engined Boeing Model 247. Based on the B-9 twin-engined bomber, the cost-effective Model 247 was equipped with wing and tail de-icing, and an aileron and elevator trim-tab system. A good deal faster than other airliners of the day, with a cruising speed of 304km/h (189mph) at 3,658m (12,000ft), the Model 247 seated 10 passengers in single seats either side of the central isle, and had a crew of two pilots plus a stewardess. There was also a galley and a toilet at the rear of the cabin.

In 1934 the famous London-to-Melbourne 'Mac-Robertson' race was won by a de Havilland D.H.88 Comet. More significantly, in second place was a KLM Royal Dutch Airlines twin-engined Douglas DC-2, fully equipped with a crew of four and three fare-paying passengers, plus a cargo of 191kg (420lb) of mail. A Boeing Model 247 came third.

One year later, in 1935, what has proved to be a most remarkable aircraft took to the skies and today, over half a century later, the immortal and seemingly irreplaceable Douglas DC-3 is still in service. The age-less DC-3 in all its various versions, including the wartime C-47 Skytrain and Dakota, also remains the most prolific of all production aircraft, with nearly 11,000 being built. With its unrivalled record of airline service, the Douglas DC3 is the earliest airline to be featured in this book and the only prewar aircraft still in airline service worldwide.

At the conclusion of World War II, only the USA were still developing civil aircraft, thereby having a tremendous advantage over the rest of the world where available production capacity had been concentrated on military aircraft. But stop-gap production conversions added to the redundant military craft, resulted in a multitude of small airlines springing up all over the globe.

Bombers such as the Halifax, Lancaster, Liberator and the Flying Fortress all underwent conversions, the most successful being the Boeing B-29 Superfortress. Developed and converted into the Stratocruiser, it led the field in the 40s.

New designs began to emerge in the late forties and early fifties for both two- and four-engined airliners. The arrival of the DC-4, 6 and 7 airliners from Douglas, plus the Constellation and Super Constellation range from Lockheed, kept the USA in the forefront of the four-engined airliner market. In the UK, under the guiding arm of the Brabazon Committee, Vickers developed the highly successful Viscount, which in the early fifties was the only propeller-turbine-powered airliner in production anywhere in the World. On the four-engined front of short/medium-range aircraft, the USA's two major types were the Martin 2-0-2 and the more successful Convair 240, which continued in production well into the sixties, while the principle UK type was the Vickers Viking. However, these were all overshadowed by the Soviet Union's Il-12 and Il-14, designed by Sergei Ilyushin. The Il-14 rivalled the DC-3 in that it was the most prolifically produced Soviet airliner used for both civil and military operations throughout the Communist bloc.

The fifties also saw the advent of the turbojet, first

on the scene being the Brabazon-designed de Havilland Comet, which entered service with BOAC in 1952. It was followed by the Soviet Union's very basic Tupolev Tarin-jet Tu-104 ('Camel') in 1956, two years ahead of the first American jetliner, the Boeing 707. It was the 707 – which first entered service with Pan American and was used on the North Atlantic route – that sparked off the jet airliner mania. The great rivalry between Pan Am and Trans World Airlines, who ordered 707s simultaneously, led airline after airline to swell Boeing's order books. Boeing took full advantage of their 12-month lead over their greatest rival, Douglas, whose DC-8 did not enter service until September 1959.

The 1950s therefore ended in a boom for both the manufacturers and the airlines. In addition, the Sud-Aviation Caravelle, the first 'clean-wing' airliner, (i.e. with a rear-mounted engine layout), entered service in 1959, leading to a vogue for aft-engined airliners in the sixties. These included the BAC One-Eleven and the McDonnell Douglas DC-9 twin-jets; tri-jets led by the Trident and the Soviet TU-154; and most importantly, the remarkable 'T'-tailed Boeing 727, the greatest-selling jet airliner in history. The 727 utilized the same fuselage cross-section as the 707 from the cabin floor upwards, and also introduced a system of wing high-lift devices which gave outstanding take-off and landing characteristics. The impact of the short/medium-haul 727 on two decades of air transport is unrivalled.

By the 1960s it was evident that the major airlines preferred jets for medium and long-haul routes because of the advantages in terms of flying time and passenger comfort. However, this was not necessarily accepted for short-haul operations, and a more cautious attitude prevailed. Boeing again led the way by starting development of the 737 as soon as the 727 was in commercial service. They were able to get the 737 into service by 1967, and a year later announced the mighty 747, the first wide-body jet, which was destined to have yet another fundamental effect upon commercial air travel.

The 747 was launched against a mood of apprehension from the world's press, who wondered if such a large aircraft was really needed and whether it might just drop out of the sky. Pan Am were the airline to

respond, with an initial order for 25. The 747 made its maiden flight in 1969 and quite literally brought a new dimension to air travel. The spacious rear, and huge number of passengers up to 500 seated ten abreast also created internal catering problems for the staff.

The 747 was thus the first of a new generation of wide-bodied airliners, and was followed one year later by the McDonnell Douglas DC-10, with maximum seating capacity of 380. In 1974 came the Lockheed Tristar, delayed due to the collapse of Rolls-Royce, who were developing the RB.211 engines, and Airbus Industrie's highly successful A300, which has a maximum high-density seating capacity of 336.

Airbus Industrie A300 the first European wide-body jet

In the last ten years the aircraft industry has continued to develop and diversify at a phenomenal rate. Concorde entered commercial service in January 1976, just over four years after the first prototype flight. A masterpiece of advanced airline technology, Concorde can cruise at above Mach 2 with 128 passengers aboard, and is powered by four Rolls-Royce Olympus engines which are grouped in pairs under its novel delta platform wings. The first supersonic airliner to fly was the Tupolev Tu-144 on 31 December 1968, but whilst Concorde remains in profitable service with British Airways and Air France, Aeroflot

British Aerospace HS 748 now in service in over 50 countries

withdrew the Tu-144 from service in 1978, following an accident to one of the fleet of 13. A third supersonic airliner was to be built by Boeing; however, their Model 2707-300 (planned to seat 250 passengers and cruise at Mach 2.7) was abandoned after the US government withdrew official backing in the early 1970s.

Other recent developments include the turboprop revolution. The British Aerospace HS748 has been in production for 28 years and, although not as successful as the Fokker F27 Friendship, in July 1986 an

British Aerospace successor to the HS 748 the BAe Advanced Turboprop (ATP)

Advanced Turboprop, the BAe ATP, had its maiden flight in preparation for scheduled service in 1987, whilst Fokker continue to produce the F27. China now manufactures the Soviet An-24 under license at their Xian works and de Havilland Canada have continued their Dash 7 STOL success with the smaller DHC-8 Dash 8. France and Italy have combined successfully to produce the high-winged ATR 42, which entered service in 1986.

Another area of intense turboprop development in the 1980s has been that of the city commuter craft. In addition to the continued development carried out by Cessna, Piper and Beech, the revived BAe

The popular British Aerospace Jetstream 31 feederliner

Jetstream 31 made its maiden flight in 1980, a year ahead of the maiden flight of the Shorts 360. The successful Brazilian organization, Empresa Brasileira de Aeronautic SA (EMBRAER), followed their EMB-110 Bandeirante in 1983 with the EMB-120 Brasilia.

Tremendous technological developments in the aircraft industry have made possible a further dimension, with fuel-efficient engines being included in total refits of McDonnell Douglas DC-9s. Forever looking to the future, McDonnell Douglas are now wind-tunnel-testing the Ultra High Bypass engines on MD-80 aircraft, using 50% less fuel than today's turbo fans. Test flights are set for 1987.

GLOSSARY

Anhedral: Downward slope of wing seen from front in direction from root to tip

APFD: Autopilot flight director

APU: Auxiliary power unit (part of aircraft)

Aspect Ratio: Measure of wing (or other aerofoil) slenderness seen in plan view, usually defined as the square of the span divided by area

Attack, Angle of: Angle at which airstream meets aerofoil (angle between mean chord and free-stream direction)

AUW: All-up weight (term meaning total weight of aircraft under defined conditions, or at specific time during flight)

Avionics: Aviation electronics, such as communications radio, radars, navigation systems and computers

BCAR: British Civil Airworthiness Requirements

BOW: Basic operating weight

BPR: Bypass ratio

Bypass Ratio: Airflow through fan duct (not passing through core) divided by airflow through core

CAA: Civil Aviation Authority (UK)

CAR: Civil Airworthiness Regulations

CFRP: Carbonfibre-reinforced plastics

Chord: Distance from leading edge to trailing edge measured parallel to longditude axis.

Clean: In-flight configuration with landing gear, flaps, slats, etc., retracted

Composite Material: Made of two constituents, or short filaments or short whiskers plus adhesive

Convertible: Transport aircraft able to be equipped to carry passengers or cargo

CR: Counter-rotating (propellers)

Dihedral: Upward slope of wing seen from front, in direction from root to tip

DINS: Digital inertial navigation system

ehp: Equivalent horsepower, measure of propulsive power of turboprop made up of shp plus addition due to residual thrust from jet

ekW: Equivalent kilowatts, SI measure of propulsive power of turboprop

Elevon: Wing trailing-edge control surface, combining functions of aileron and elevator

EPU: Emergency power unit (part of aircraft, not used for propulsion)

FAA: Federal Aviation Agency

FAR: Federal Aviation

14

Regulations

Feathering: Setting propeller or similar blades at pitch aligned with slipstream, to give resultant torque (not tending to turn shaft) and thus minimum drag

Field Length: Measure of distance needed to land and/or take off: many different measures for particular purposes, each precisely defined

Flaperon: Wing trailing-edge surface combining functions of flap and aileron

Flat-Four: Engine having four horizontally opposed cylinders: thus, flat-twin, flat-six, etc.

Flat Rated: Propulsion engine capable of giving full thrust or power for take-off up to high airfield height and/or high ambient temperature (thus, probably derated at S/L)

Fly by Wire: Flight control system with electrical signalling (i.e. without mechanical interconnection between cockpit flying controls and control surfaces)

Fowler Flap: Moves initially aft to increase wing area and then also deflects down to increase drag

Gallon: Non-SI measure; 1 Imp gal (UK) = 4.546 litres; 1 US gal = 3.785 litres

h: Hours

hp: Horsepower

IAS: Indicated airspeed

IATA: International Air Transport Association

ICAO: International Civil Aviation Organization

ILS: Instrument landing system

Incidence: Strictly, the angle at which the wing is set in relation to the fore/aft axis. Wrongly used to mean angle of attack.

Integral Tank: Fuel or other liquid tank formed by sealing part of structure

km/h: Kilometres per hour

knot: 1nm per hour

kW: Kilowatt, SI measure of all forms of power (not just electrical)

lbf: Pounds of thrust

m: Metre(s), SI unit of length

M or Mach number: The ratio of the speed of a body to the speed of sound (1,116ft/sec or 340m/sec in air at 15°C) under the same ambient conditions

MLW: Maximum landing weight

mm: Millimetres

Monocoque: Structure with strength in outer shell, devoid of internal bracing

mph: Miles per hour

MZFW: Maximum zero-fuel weight

nm: Nautical mile, 1.8532km, 1.15152mls

Payload: Disposable load generating revenue

(passengers, cargo, mail and other paid items)

Plane: A lifting surface (e.g. wing, tailplane)

Port: Left side, looking forward

Primary Flight Controls: Those used to control trajectory of aircraft (thus, not trimmers, tabs, flaps, slats, air brakes or lift dumpers, etc.)

Radius: In terms of performance, the distance an aircraft can fly from base and return without intermediate landing

Rafanned: Gas-turbine engine fitted with new fan of higher BPR

Range: The distance an aircraft can fly (or is permitted to fly) with specified load and usually whilst making allowance for specified additional manoeuvres

Service Ceiling: Usually height equivalent to air density at which maximum attainable rate of climb is 100ft/min

Servo: A device which acts as a relay, usually augmenting the pilot's efforts to move a control surface or the like

shp: Shaft horsepower, measure of power transmitted via rotating shaft

S/L: Sea level

st: Static thrust

Stabilizer: Fin (thus, horizontal stabilizer = tailplane)

Stalling Speed: TAS at which aircraft stalls at 1g, i.e. wing lift suddenly collapses

Starboard: Right side, looking forward

STOL: Short take-off and landing. (Several definitions, stipulating allowable horizontal distance to clear screen height of 35 or 50ft or various SI measures)

Supercritical wing: Wing of relatively deep, flat-topped profile generating lift right across upper surface instead of concentrated close behind leading edge

Sweepback: Backward inclination of wing or other aerofoil, seen from above, measured relative to fuselage or other reference axis, usually measured at quarter-chord (25%) or at leading-edge

t: Tonne, 1 Megagram, 1,000kg

Taileron: Left and right tailplanes used as primary control surfaces in both pitch and roll

Tailplane: Main horizontal tail surface, originally fixed and carrying hinged elevator(s), but today often a single 'slab' serving as control surface

TAS: True airspeed, EAS (estimated airspeed) corrected for density (often very large factor) appropriate to aircraft height

T-O: Take-off

TOGW: Take-off gross weight

ton: Imperial (long) ton = 1.016t (Mg), US (short) ton = 0.9072t

Turbofan: Gas-turbine jet engine generating most thrust by a large-diameter cowled fan, with small part added by jet from core

Turbojet: Simplest form of gas turbine comprising compressor, combustion chamber, turbine and propulsive nozzle

Turboprop: Gas turbine in which as much energy as possible is taken from gas jet and used to drive reduction gearbox and propeller

Turboshaft: Gas turbine in which as much energy as possible is taken from gas jet and used to drive high-speed shaft (which in turn drives external load such as helicopter gearbox)

VMO: Maximum permitted operating flight speed (IAS, EAS or CAS must be specified).

Wing Area: Total projected area of clean wing including all control surfaces and area of fuselage bounded by leading and trailing edges projected to centreline

Winglet: Small auxiliary aerofoil, usually sharply upturned and often swept back, at tip of wing

ZFW: Zero-fuel weight

Aircraft production figures were accurate at the time of going to press but would, in many instances, have altered since.

AEROSPATIALE CARAVELLE

Country of Origin: France

Production: Number built 280; in airline service 76
Power Plant: Two 5,725kgp (12,600lb st) Rolls-Royce
Avon 532R or 533R turbojets

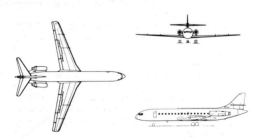

Performance: Max cruising speed at 7,620m (25,000ft), 845km/h (525mph); range with max payload 2,300km (1,430mls)

Weights: Basic operating weight 28,655kg (63,175lb); max payload 8,200kg (18,080lb); max take-off weight 50,000kg (110,230lb)

Dimensions: Span 34.30m (112ft 7in); length 32.01m (105ft 0in); height 8.72m (28ft 7in); wing area 146.7m² (1,579sq ft)

Seating capacity: 64

History: The Caravelle was one of the first turbojet-engined purpose-designed short-to-medium range aircraft. Prototype test flights commenced on May 1955 and Air France placed the first order for 12 in November 1955. The aircraft entered regular service on 6 May 1959.

AEROSPATIALE CORVETTE 100

Country of Origin: France
Production: Number built 40: in airline service 30
Power Plant: Two 1,048kgp (2,310lb st) Pratt & Whitney (VALL) JT 15D-4 turbofans

Performance: Max cruising speed 796km/h (495mph) at 9,144m (30,000ft); best economy cruise 630km/h (391mph) at 11,000m (36,100ft); initial rate of climb 15.25m/sec (3,000ft/min); service ceiling 11,580m (38,00ft); range with max payload 1,645km (1,022mls); range with max fuel 2,690km (1,670mls)
Weights: Empty equipped 3,622kg (7,985lb); max

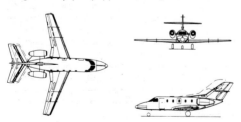

payload 1,020kg (2,248lb); max take-off 6,100kg (13,450lb)

Dimensions: Span 12.80m (42ft 0in); length 13.82m (45ft 4in); height 4.23m (13ft 10in);
wing area 22.0m² (236.8sq ft)

Seating capacity: 12

History: The first prototype flew on 16 July 1970, with a second prototype on 20 December 1970 and a third in March 1973. Although the first production aircraft flew on 9 November 1973, deliveries were seriously delayed by strikes at the Canadian plant manufacturing the engines, and the Corvette did not enter service with Air Alps until September 1974. Wing-tip tanks could be added to extend the range. Plans to develop a stretched fuselage variant, the Corvette 200, were never put into operation, and production ceased in 1977.

AEROSPATIALE NORD 262 Fregate

Country of Origin: France
Production: Number built 110; in airline service 32
Power Plant: Two 1,145ehp Turbomeca Bastan VII turbo props

AIR LIMOUSIN T.A

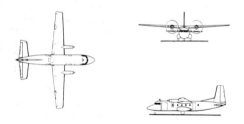

Performance: Max speed 385km/h (239mph); cruising speed 375km/h (233mph); initial rate of climb 6.1m/sec (1,200ft/min); service ceiling 7,160m (23,500ft);

range with max payload 975km (605mls); range with max fuel 1,760km (1,095mls)

Weights: Basic operating weight 7,029kg (15,496lb); max payload 3,270kg (7,209lb); max take-off weight 10,600kg (23,370lb); max landing 10,300kg (22,710lb)

Dimensions: Span (N262 A) 21.90m (71ft 10in); Span (Fregate) 22.60m (74ft 1.75in); length 19.28m (63ft 3in); height 6.20m (20ft 4in); wing area (N262 A) 55.0m² (592sq ft); wing area (Fregate) 55.79m² (601sq ft)

Seating capacity: 24-26

History: The Nord 262 was a development of the Nord Aviation MH-260 (which first flew 29 July 1960), the new feature being a pressurized circular-section fuselage. The Nord 262 B entered service with Air Inter on 16 July 1964. The 262 A entered service in August 1965.

23

AEROSPATIALE C-160 TRANSALL

Country of Origin: France/Germany
Production: Number ordered (civil version) 11; in airline service 11
Power Plant: Two Rolls-Royce Type RTY 20 MK22 turboprops each rated at 6,200ehp for take-off
Performance: Max speed 592km/h (367mph) at 4,875m

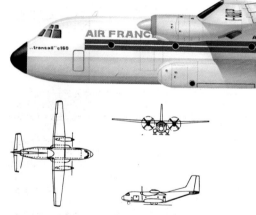

(16,000ft); economical cruising speed 454km/h (282mph) at 6,100m (20,000ft); rate of climb 6.6m/sec (1,300ft/min); service ceiling 7,770m (25,500ft); range 4,800km (2,982mls) with 8,000kg (17,637lb) payload,

and 1,700km (1,056mls) with 16,000kg (35,274lb)
Dimensions: Span 40.0m (13ft 3in); length 32.4m (106ft 3.5in); height 12.36m (40ft 6.75in); wing area 160.10m² (1,723sq ft)
History: Developed for both the German and French military, the first prototype flight was on 25 February 1963. Assembly lines were set up in both countries and by 1970 about 170 aircraft had been produced, including 9 for the South African Air Force. SOGERMA converted four of the C-160Fs of the Armée de L'Air for Air France. These were redesignated as C-160P and operate between Paris and Bastia (Corsica) for mail carrying. They average 13.5 tons (1.8 million letters) nightly, loading and off-loading in about 12 minutes.

AEROSPATIALE AERITALIA ATR42-200

Country of Origin: France/Italy

Production: Number ordered 60; in airline service 10 (50)

Power Plant: 2 x 1,800shp PWAC PW 120 turboprops

Performance: Max cruising speed 509km/h (316mph) at 6,100m (20,000ft); range with max payload 2,420km

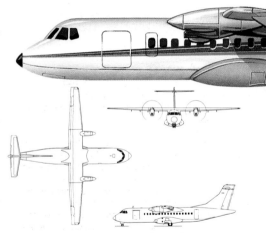

(1,500mls); range with max fuel 5,566km (3,457mls)

Weights: Rump weight, 15,770kg (34,767lb); max take-off weight 15,570kg (34,723lb); max landing weight

15,500kg (34,175lb); empty 9,609kg (21,184lb)
Dimensions: Span 24.57m (80ft 6in); length
22.7m (74ft 5in); height 7.59m (24ft 9 in); wing area
54.5m² (586sq ft)
Seating capacity: 46
History: The ATR42 entered service in 1986 in South
Europe and North America after both French and
Italian government-owned manufacturers signed an
agreement in 1979. Aeritalia is responsible for the
design and manufacture of the fuselage and the tail,
with the final assembly being made in Toulouse. Production rate was increased to three per month at the
end of 1986 and this has now been raised to four per
month. In addition to the 60 orders, there already
exist offers for a further 38, including the ATR42-300
which has a higher gross weight.

AEROSPATIALE AERITALIA ATR 72

Country of Origin: France/Italy
Production: Number ordered and on option 21
Power Plant: 2 x Pratt & Whitney Canada pur-124-2
turboprops

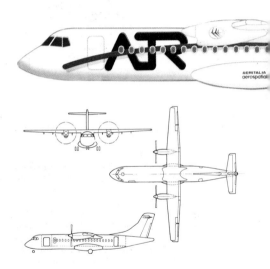

Performance: Max cruising speed 530km/h (330mph); max range 2,778km (1,725mls)

Weights: Empty 12,200kg (26,931lb); max take-off weight 19,990-21,500kg (44,128-47,461lb) **Dimensions:** Span 27.05m (88ft 9in); length 27.16m (89ft 1in); height 7.65m (25ft 1in)

Seating capacity: 64-72

History: The first flight is scheduled for May 1988, exactly three years after Aerospatiale and Aeritalia announced their plans to launch a stretched fuselage version of the ATP 142. The 21 orders are from both European and North American airlines, the first of them being placed by Finnair. Design work is now complete and the prototype is under construction.

AEROSPATIALE/BRITISH AEROSPACE CONCORDE

Country of Origin: France/United Kingdom

Production: Number built 16; in airline service 14

Power Plant: Four 17,260kgp (38,050lb st) Rolls-Royce/SNECMA Olympus 593 Mk 610 turbojets with silencers and reversers

Performance: Max cruising speed at 16,600m (54,500ft), 2,333km/h (1,450mph); best range cruise, Mach 2.50; service ceiling about 18,288m (60,000ft); range with max payload 4,900km (3,050mls); range with max fuel, 7,215km (4,490mls)

Weights: Basic operating weight 77,110kg (170,000lb); typical payload 11,340kg (25,000lb); max take-off 181,400kg (400,000lb); max landing 108,860kg (240,000lb)

Dimensions: Span 25.60m (85ft 0in); length 62.17m (203ft 11.5in); height 12.19m (40ft 0in); wing area 358.25m² (3,856sq ft)

Seating capacity: 128

History: It took 20 years from the establishing of the Supersonic Transport Aircraft Committee in 1956 to Concorde's first scheduled supersonic service. France joined in the project on 29 November 1962; since then all production has alternated on two lines, at Toulouse and Filton. Prototype Concorde 001 first flew on 2 March 1969, and the Filton-assembled 002 on 9 April 1969. Further prototypes, 101 and 102, were first flown on 17 December 1971 and 10 January 1973 respectively, and 201 and 202 on 6 December 1973 and 13 February 1974 respectively. British Airways inaugurated their scheduled service between London and Bahrain on 16 January 1976; on the same day, Air France opened their routes from Paris to Dakar and Rio De Janeiro. Transatlantic flights from London and Paris to Washington (Dulles) began on 24 May 1976, and the all-important New York route was opened in December 1977.

31

AIRBUS INDUSTRIE A300 B2

Country of Origin: European
Production: Number ordered 270; in airline service 250 (14)
Power Plant: Two General Electric CF6-50A turbo fans rated at 23,133kgp (51,000lb st)
Performance: Maximum operating speed 666km/h

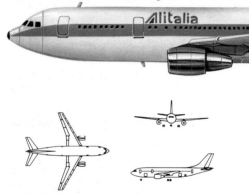

(413mph); range 1,668km (1,035mls) with max payload; range with max fuel, 3,700km (2,300mls)
Weights: Operating empty 84,810g (186,980lb); max structural payload 31,690kg (69,850lb); max usable fuel 34,500kg (76,000lb); max take-off weight

142,000kg (313,055lb); max landing weight 130,000kg (286,600lb); max zero fuel weight 120,500kg (265,655lb)

Dimensions: Span 44.84m (147ft 1in); length 53.62m (175ft 11in); height 16.53m (54ft 2in); wing area 260m² (2,800sq ft)

Seating capacity: 281

History: The first European production of a 'wide body' short-to-medium range airliner, the A300 entered service with Air France in 1974. Initiated as an Anglo-French project in 1965, the UK government withdrew from the project in early 1969 due to lack of orders, although Hawker Siddeley retained their responsibility for the design and production of the wing. Later that year both Spain and the Netherlands joined the project. The British government reentered the project on 1 January 1979.

AIRBUS INDUSTRIE A310 - 202

Country of Origin: European
Production: Number ordered 117; in airline service 69 (47)
Power Plant: Two General Electric CF6-80A turbofans of 21,800kgp (48,000lb st) each; fuel capacity 43,039kg (94,800lb)

Performance: Cruising speed Mach — 0.78 at 10.668m (35,000ft), ISA; take-off field length, max weight, 1981m (6,500ft); approach speed at max landing weight 246 km/h (133ft); range with 234 passengers

and baggage, 4815km (2,600n mls); range with max payload 1870km (1,550n mls)

Weights: Operating weight empty 76,469kg (168,434lb); max payload 32,400kg (71,500lb); max take-off 132,000kg (291,010lb); max landing 118,500kg (261,250lb); max zero fuel 108,500kg (239,200lb)

Dimensions: Span 43.90m (144ft 0in); length 46.66m 153ft 1in); height 15.80m (51ft 10in); wing area 219.0m^2 (2,35 sq ft)

Seating capacity: 214

History: Designed with a shorter fuselage than the A300, the A310 also incorporated a new wing design and smaller tail plane. The first orders were obtained from Swissair, who commenced service with them early in 1983.

AIRBUS INDUSTRIE A320

Country of Origin: European
Production: Number ordered 269; in airline service 0
(269)
Power Plant: Two 10,680-11,360kg (23,500 - 25,000lb)
CFM 56-5 or IAE V2500 turbofans

Performance: Max cruise speed at 8,530m (28,000ft) 903km/h (560mph); range 3,450km (2,143mls)

Weights: Operating weight empty 38,180kg (84,170lb); max take-off 61,000kg (134,500lb); max landing 57,000kg (125,700lb); max payload 18,840kg (41,530lb)

Dimensions: Span 33.91m (111ft 3in); length 37.57m (123ft 3in); height 11.76m (38ft 7in); wing area 122.4m² (1,318sq ft)

Seating capacity: 179 max

History: The first flight is scheduled for Spring 1987 with delivery due to start a year later. With development costs estimated at $1.7 billion (£1,130m), 600 aircraft will have to be built to reach a breakeven point; so far over 250 have been ordered, with options on a further 150 plus.

ANTONOV An-12

Country of Origin: Soviet Union
Production: Number built 850 plus; in airline service 212 plus
Power Plant: Four 4,000ehp Ivchenko A1-20k turboprops
Performance: Max speed 715km/h (444mph); max

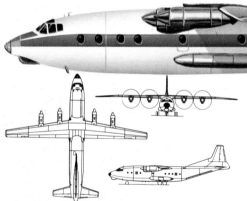

cruise 600km/h (373mph); normal cruise 550km/h (342mph) at 7,500m (25,000ft); initial climb rate 10.0m/sec (1,970ft/min); service ceiling 10,200m (33,500ft); range 3,400km (2,110mls) with 10,000kg (22,050lb) payload and one hour reserves

Weights: Empty 28,000kg (61,730lb); normal loaded 54,000kg (119,050lb); max take-off 61,000kg

Dimensions: Span 38.00m (124ft 8in); length 37.00m (121ft 4.5in); height 9.83m (32ft 3in); wing area 119.5m² (1,286sq ft)

History: Developed from the An-10A as a commercial freighter primarily for the military, the An-12 proved to be very successful and is still flown extensively by Aeroflot and a few other commercial airlines. Besides the integral loading ramp and a heavy-duty freight floor capable of withstanding weights of 1,500kg/sq m (307lb/sq ft), the An-12 military version also had a tail gun turret which was glazed over in the early civilian An-12V model and finally replaced in late production models by a fairing.

ANTONOV An-22
Country of Origin: Soviet Union

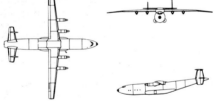

Production: Number built 100 plus; in airline service 48 plus
Power Plant: Four 15,000shp Kuznetsov NK - 12MA turboprops

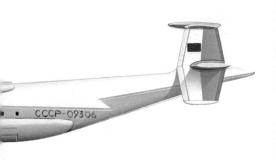

Performance: Max speed 740km/h (460mph); max cruise 679km/h (422mph); range (with max payload - 80,000kg/176,350lb) 5,000km (3,107mls); range (with max fuel and 45,000kg/99,200lb payload) 10,950km (6,800mls); cruising altitude 8,000-10,000m (26,250-32,800ft)

Weights: Empty equipped 114,000kg (251,327lb); max take-off 250,000kg (551,156lb)

Dimensions: Span 64.40m (211ft 3.5in); length 57.80m (189ft 8in); height 12.53m (41ft 1in); wing area 345m² (3,713.6sq ft)

Seating capacity: 28

History: Developed as a heavy military and commercial freighter, the An-22 first flew on 27 February 1965 and was then the world's largest aircraft. The main hold contains four travelling gantries and two winches each with a 2500kg (5500lb) capacity.

ANTONOV An-24V

Country of Origin: Soviet Union

Production: Number built 1,100 plus; in airline service 864 plus

Power Plant: Two 2,500ehp Ivchenko A1-24 Seriiny II turboprops

POLSKIE LINIE LOTNICZE·LOT·

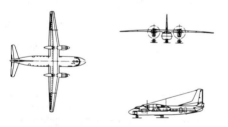

Performance: Max cruise 498km/h (310mph); best range cruise 450km/h (280mph) at 6,000m (19,700ft);

initial climb 7.7m/sec (1,515ft/min); service ceiling 8,400m (27,560ft); range (max payload and reserves) 550km (341mls); (max fuel and 45min reserves) 2,400km (1,490mls)

Weights: Empty 13,300kg (29,320lb); max take-off 21,000kg (46,300lb)

Dimensions: Span 29.20m (95ft 9.5in); length 23.53m (77ft 2.5in); height 8.32m (27ft 3.5in); wing area 74.98m² (807.1sq ft)

Seating capacity: 50

History: First flown in 1960, the An-24 entered service with Aeroflot in September 1963. Today Aeroflot have more An-24s than any other aircraft. Production continued until 1977, including the specialized freighters An-24T and An-24RT. The aircraft is still flown by 15 airlines.

ANTONOV An-28

Country of Origin: Soviet Union
Production: Number built 15 plus; in airline service 15 plus

Power Plant: Two 970shp Glushenkar TDV-10B turboprops
Performance: Max cruising speed 350km/h (217mph);

CCCP-48105

initial rate of climb 12.0m/sec (2,360ft/min); range with max payload 1,000km (620mls); range with max fuel 1,300km (805mls)

Weights: Max payload 1,550kg (3,415lb); max take-off weight 6,100kg (13,450lb)

Dimensions: Span 21.99m (72ft 7in); length 12.98m (42ft 7in); height 4.60m (15ft 1in); wing area 39.72m² (427.5sq ft)

Seating capacity: 15

History: Although first flown in September 1969, production models were not seen until 1974. A larger derivative of the An-14 which first flew in 1958, the An-28 has hinged-wing trailing edges, and wide-tread low-pressure balloon tyres which enable the aircraft to use short rough airstrips of 550-600m (600-650yds). Production continues at the Polish P2L company's Meilec factory.

ANTONOV AN-30
Country of Origin: USSR
Power Plant: Two 2,103kw (2,820ehp) Ivcheuko

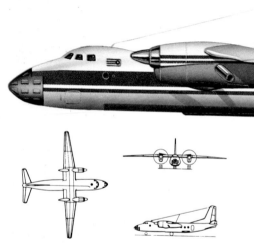

A1-24VT turboprop engines, with water injection
Performance: Max speed 540km/h (335mph); service
ceiling 8,300m (27,230ft); range with max fuel
2,630km (1,634mls)

Weights: Basic operating 15,590kg (34,370lb); max take-off and landing 23,000kg (50,705lb)

Dimensions: Span 29.20m (95ft 9.5in); length 24.26m (79ft 7in); height 8.32m (27ft 3.5in); wing area 74.98m² (807.1sq ft)

History: First displayed in 1977 the AN-30 was developed from the An-24RT rear loading transport aircraft which enjoyed only limited success due to the inability to load large cargoes. The AN-30 was initially employed in a survey role for the research of mineral resources, and features an extensively glazed nose and central ports for photographic equipment.

47

ANTONOV An-72

Country of Origin: Soviet Union
Production: Figures not available
Power Plant: Two 6,500kgp (14,330lb) Lotarev D-36 high bypass turbofans

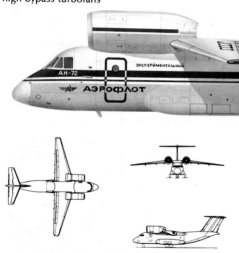

Performance: Max cruising speed 720km/h (447mph); max operating altitude 11,000m (36,090ft); Normal operating altitude 8,000-10,000m (26,250-32,800ft); take-off distance at max weight 1,200m (4,000ft);

CCCP-83966

range with max payload 1,000km (620mls); range with max fuel 3,200km (1,990mls)

Weights: Max take-off 30,500kg (67,240lb); take-off weight for 1,000m (3,280ft) runway 26,500kg (58,420lb); max payload 7,500kg (16,534lb)

Dimensions: Span 25.83m (84ft 9in); length 26.58m (87ft 2.5in); height 8.24m (27ft 0in)

History: The An-72 'Loader' first flew in late 1977 in Aeroflot markings, although it is seen as a specialized cargo transport. The two engines are located forward and above the wing which, combined with the trailing edge flaps, produce increased lift and enable the aircraft to operate off short runways. The double main wheels are on separate legs, enabling greater use of unprepared runways. A stretched version, the An-74, is now entering production.

BAC VANGUARD Type 953

Country of Origin: United Kingdom

Production: Number built 44; number in airline service 7

Power Plant: Four 5,545ehp Rolls-Royce Type 512 turboprops

Performance: High speed cruise 684km/h (425mph) at

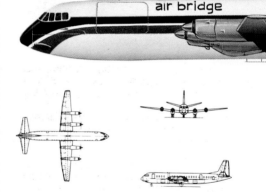

6,100m (20,000ft); long range cruise, 670km/h (420mph) at 7,620m (25,000ft); initial rate of climb 13.7m/sec (2,700ft/min); service ceiling 9,145m (30,000ft); range with max payload 2,945km (1,830mls) at plus 620m (25,000ft); range with max fuel 4,990km (3,100mls) at 7,620m (25,000ft)

G-APEG

Weights: Empty equipped 37,422kg (82,500lb); max payload 16,785kg (37,000lb); max take-off load 66,448kg (146,500lb); max landing 61,238kg (130,500lb)

Dimensions: Span 36.15m (118ft 7in); length 37.45m (122ft 10.5in); height 10.64m (34ft 11in); wing area 142.0m² (1529sq ft)

Seating capacity: 120

History: The V.V.951 first flew on 20 January 1959. However, it suffered enormous delays due to a defect in the Type 512 engine and did not enter service with BEA until March 1961. Already uncompetitive by the time it entered service, no further orders were obtained other than the initial launch order from BEA and an order from TLA, now Air Canada, placed in January 1975. The Vanguard 953 first flew on May 1961 and deliveries were completed on 30 March 1962.

51

BAC (VICKERS) SUPER VC10
Country of Origin: United Kingdom

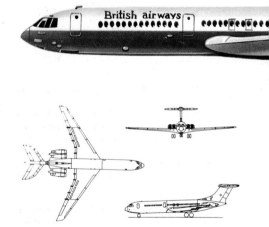

Power Plant: Four 9,888kgp (21,800lb) RCo 43D MK 550 turbofans

Performance: High speed cruise 935km/h (581mph) at 9,450m (31,000ft); long range cruise 886km/h (550mph) at 11,600m (38,000ft); range with max

payload 7,600km (4,720mls); range with max fuel 11,470km (7,128mls)

Weights: Operating weight empty 71,940kg (158,594lb); max take-off 151,950kg (335,000lb); max payload 27,360kg (60,321lb); max landing 107,500kg (237,000lb)

Dimensions: Span 44.55m (146ft 2in); length 52.32m (171ft 8in); height 12.04m (39ft 6in); wing area 272.4m² (2,932sq ft)

Seating capacity: Up to 187

History: The VC10 was the world's first rear-engined long-range intercontinental jet transport, making its first flight on 29 June 1962. It entered service with BOAC on 29 April 1964 on the London-Lagos route. The Super VC10 first flew on 7 May 1964 and entered service with BOAC on 1 April 1965. The Super VC10 was 3.96m (13ft 0in) longer and capable of carrying an additional 35 passengers.

BEECH 99A AIRLINER

Country of Origin: USA
Production: Number built 164
Power Plant: Two 680shp Pratt & Whitney PT6A-27 turbo fans

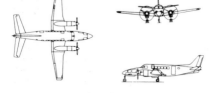

Performance: Max cruising speed 455km/h (283mph) at 2,440m (8,000ft); initial rate of climb 10.6m/sec (2,090ft/min); service ceiling 8,020m (26,313ft); range with max payload 853km (530mls); range with max

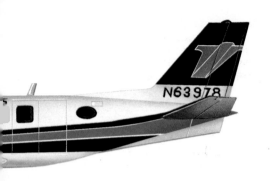

fuel 1,348m (838mls)

Weights: Empty equipped 2,663kg (5,872lb); max take-off 4,944kg (10,900lb)

Dimensions: Span 14.00m (45ft 10.5in); length 13.58m (44ft 6.75in); height 4.38m (14ft 4.25in); wing area 25.98m² (279.7sq ft)

Seating capacity: 15

History: When it first entered production in 1968, the Beech 99 Airliner was the largest of the company's twin-engined aircraft. It was basically a long-fuselage variant of the Queen Air and first flew in December 1965, with PT6A-20 turboprops being fitted in July 1966. Later 99A models were fitted with PT6A-27 turbofan engines. Production, terminated in the mid-1970s, was started again in 1980 with the launch of the C99, which is powered by PT6A-34 engines.

BEECH KING AIR C90

Country of Origin: USA
Production: Number built 1000 plus
Power Plant: Two Pratt & Whitney (Canada) PT6A-12 turboprops, each rated at 550ehp for take-off
Performance: Max cruising speed 412km/h (256m/h) at

3,660m (12,000ft); initial rate of climb 9.9m/sec (1,955ft/min); service ceiling 8,565m (28,100ft); range with max fuel 1,773-2,227km (1,100-1,384mls)

depending on altitude; max range 2,374km (1,475mls) at 6,400m (21,000ft)

Weights: Empty 2,558kg (5,640lb); max take-off 4,377kg (9,650lb)

Dimensions: Span 15.32m (50ft 3in); length 10.82m (35ft 6in); height 4.33m (14ft 2.5in); wing area 27.3m² (293.9sq ft)

Seating capacity: 6

History: A variant of the Beech Queen Air, but powered by turboprop engines and with a pressurized cabin, the first prototype flew on 20 January 1964. Designated model 90 and powered by PT6A-6 engines, it was superceded by the A90 and B90, both powered by PT6A-20s. They were followed by the C90 in 1977. All variants were of similar dimensions and capable of seating 15 in high-density layout.

BEECH SUPER KING AIR B200
Country of Origin: USA

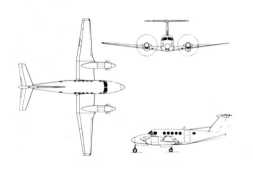

Power plant: Two 850shp Pratt & Whitney (Canada) PT6A-42 turboprops

Performance: Max cruise speed 536km/h (289ft) at 7,820m (25,000ft); range with max payload 1,418km (880mls); range with max fuel 3,570km (2,217mls)

Weights: Max take-off 5,670kg (12,500lb); max landing 5,670kg (12,500lb); empty operating 3,419kg (7,538lb)

Dimension: Span 16.61m (54ft 7in); length 13.34m (43ft 9in); height 4.75m (15ft); wing area 28.15m² (303sq ft)

Seating Capacity: 10

History: First flown on 27 October 1972, the King Air is used both as a business turboprop and as an airliner on low-density long-distance routes. The 200 has a greater wing span than the 100 and was the first Beech craft to have a T-tail; it entered service in December 1973. A civil cargo version became available in 1979.

59

BEECH Super H 18
Country of Origin: USA

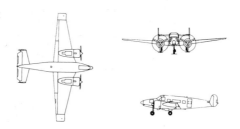

Production: Number built 9,000 plus
Power Plant: Two 450hp Pratt & Whitney R-985AN-14B
Wasp Jr piston radial engines

Performance: Max cruising speed 354km/h (220mph) at 3,050m (10,000ft); best economy cruise 298km/h (185mph) at 3,050m (10,000ft); initial rate of climb 7.1m/sec (1,400ft/min); service ceiling 6,520m (21,400ft); range with max fuel 2,460km (1,530mls)

Weights: Basic operating 2,657kg (5,845lb); max take-off 4,490kg (9,900lb)

Dimensions: Span 15.14m (49ft 8in); length 10.70m (35ft 2.5in); height 2.84m (9ft 4in); wing area 33.54m² (360.7sq ft)

Seating Capacity: 7-9

History: First flown in 1937, production lasted until 1969 and many remain in service still with air taxi operators world-wide. The Super H 18 was the last production variant but there have been a considerable number of conversion schemes, many featuring stretched fuselages which provided passenger accommodation of up to 14.

BEECH 1900C
Country of Origin: USA

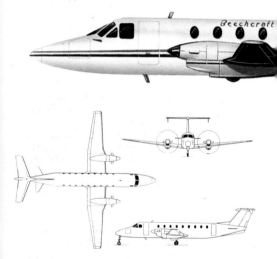

Production: Number in airline service 50
Power Plant: Two 4,000hr TBO Pratt & Whitney PT 6A-65B turboprops flat rated at 1,100shp

NI900A

Performance: Max cruise speed 473km/h (255mph) at 4,267m (14,000ft); range with max payload 1,680km (906nm); range with max fuel 1,863km (1,157mls)

Weights: Max ramp weight 7,590kg (16,710lbs); max zero fuel weight 6,349kg (14,000lb); empty weight 3,946kg (8,700lb); max take-off weight 7,540kg (16,600lb)

Dimensions: Span 16.61m (54ft 5in); length 17.65m (57ft 9in); height 4.54m (14ft 9in); wing area 28.16m² (303sq ft)

Seating Capacity: 19

History: First flown in September 1982, the Beech 1900C airliner has taken over from the C99, production of which has now been run down. The airliner offers excellent baggage facilities and loadability with the option of loading full fuel and payload simultaneously without exceeding the maximum take-off weight.

BOEING 707-320C

Country of Origin: USA
Production: Number built 828; in airline service 270
Power Plant: Four 8,165kgp (18,000lb st) Pratt & Whitney JT3D-3 or 8,618kgp (19,000lb st) JT3D-7 turbofans
Performance: Max cruising speed 965km/h (600mph); best economy cruise 886km/h (550mph); initial rate of

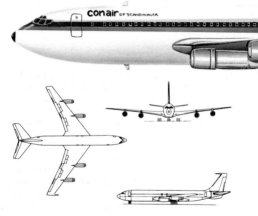

climb 20.3m/sec (4,000ft/min); service ceiling 11,885M (39,000ft); range with max payload 6,920km (4,300mls); range with max fuel 12,030km (7,475mls)

Weight: Basic operating 62,872-66,224kg (136,610-146,000lb); max payload (passenger) 38,100kg (84,000lbs), (cargo) 41,453kg (91,390lbs); max take-off 151,315kg (333,600lb)

Dimensions: Span 44.42m (145ft 8.5in); length 45.6m (152ft 11in); height 12.94m (42ft 5.5in); wing area 283.4m^2 (3,050sq ft)

Seating Capacity: Up to 189 in one class

History: The Boeing 707 first entered service on 26 October 1958 with Pan American between London and New York and was the first US-built commercial jet transport. It had taken Boeing six years from making the decision to proceed with the building of the prototype, which they first flew on 15 July 1954. The 707 thereby heralded a revolution in international passenger jet travel.

BOEING 720B

Country of Origin: USA
Production: Number built 154; in airline service 30
Power Plant: Four 7,718kgp (17,000lb st) Pratt & Whitney JT3D-1 or 8165kgp (18,000lb st) JT3D-3 turbofans

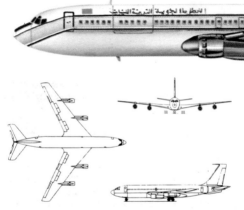

Performance: Max cruising speed at 7,620m (25,000ft), 978km/h (608mph); best economy cruise 858km/h (533mph); initial rate of climb 18.7m/sec (3,700ft/min); service ceiling 12,344m (40,500ft); range with max payload 6,614km (4,110mls); range with max fuel

10,380km (6,450mls)

Weights: Empty operating 52,136km (115,000lb); max payload 18,600kg (41,000lb); max take-off 106,140kg (233,508lb)

Dimensions: Span 39.87m (130ft 10in); length 41.68m (136ft 9in); height 12.67m (41ft 7in); wing area 234.2m^2 (2,521sq ft)

Seating capacity: 149

History: An aerodynamically refined short-to-medium range variant of the 707. The Boeing 720 first flew on 23 November 1959 and entered service with both United and American in July 1960. The introduction of the front fan version of the JT3c Pratt & Whitney engine added greater power and lower fuel consumption and the resultant aircraft, designated 720B, entered service with American in March 1961.

BOEING 727-200

Country of Origin: USA

Production: Number built 1,831; in airline service 1,658

Power Plant: Three 6,804kgp (15,000lb st) Pratt & Whitney JT8D-11 or 7,030kgp (15,500lb st) JT8D-15 or 7,257kgp (16,000lb st) JT8D-17 turbofans

Performance: Max cruising speed 964km/h (599mls/h)

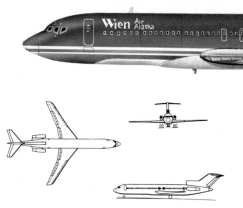

at 7,530m (24,700ft); economy cruise 917km/h (570mph) at 9,145m (30,000ft); initial rate of climb 13.2m/sec (2,600ft/min); service ceiling 10,210m

(33,500ft); range with max payload over 4,500km (over 2,800mls)

Weights: Operating weight empty 45,360kg (100,000lb); max payload 19,414kg (42,800lb); max take-off 95,027kg (209,500lb)

Dimensions: Span 32.92m (108ft 0in); length 46.69m (153ft 2in); height 10.36m (34ft 0in); wing area 157.9m² (1,700sq ft)

Seating Capacity: 125

History: First ordered by United and Eastern in 1960, the 727 eventually became the world's best selling jet airliner and is now still operated by over 100 airlines. First flown on 9 February 1963, the 727 entered service with Eastern in February 1964. The 727-200 is the stretched version, some 20ft longer, and first entered service on 14 December 1967 with Northern Airlines.

BOEING 737-200

Country of Origin: USA

Production: Number ordered 1,532; in airline service 1,086 (342)

Power Plant: Two 6,350kgp (14,000lb st) Pratt & Whitney JT8D-7 or 6,577kgp (14,400lb st) JT8D-9 or 7,030kgp (15,500lb st) JT8D-15 turbofans

Performance: Max cruising speed 927km/h (576mph) at 6,890m (22,600ft); best economy cruise 890km/h (553mph); initial rate of climb 19.1m/sec (3,760ft/

min); range with max payload 3,851km (2,370mls); range with max fuel 4.075km (2,530mls)

Dimensions: Span 28.35m (93ft 0in); length 30.48m (100ft 0in); height 11.28m (37ft 0in); wing area 91.05m² (980sq ft)

Seating Capacity: 119

History: Boeing's short-haul airliner entered service behind the BAC One-Eleven and the DC-9 with the first order coming from Lufthansa in February 1965. Boeing kept the same overall fuselage width as the 707 and the 727 but opted for under-wing engines as opposed to their competitors' tail arrangement. The stretched 737-200, 1.82m (6ft) longer, entered service with United on 28 April 1968.

BOEING 747-200
Country of Origin: USA

Production: Number ordered 671; in airline service 598 (46)

Power Plant: Four 19,730kgp (43,500lb st) Pratt & Whitney JT9D-3, or 20,410kgp (45,000lb st) JT9D-3W, or 20,635kgp (45,500lb st) JT9D-7 or 21,320kgp (47,000lb st) JT9D-7W or 21,620kgp (47,670lb st) JT9D-7A turbofans

Performance: Max speed 978km/h (608mph) at 9,150m (30,000ft); best economy cruise 935km/h (580mph); cruise ceiling 13,705m (45,000ft); range with max payload 8,023km (4,985mls); range with max fuel 11,410km (7,090mls)

Weights: Basic operating 166,876kg (367,900lb); max payload 71,940kg (158,600lb); max take-off 356,070kg (785,000lb)

Dimensions: Span 59.64m (195ft 8in); length 70.51m

(231ft 4in); height 19.33m (63ft 5in); wing area 511m² (5,500sq ft)

Seating Capacity: 350

History: The largest airliner in service, the 'Jumbo Jet' was also the first of the wide-bodied jets into service. Initial orders were placed by Pan American but this had grown to over 27 airlines by the time of the first

flight on 9 February 1969. The 747 entered service with Pan American on 21 January 1970 on the trans-atlantic route. The 747-200 has the same overall dimensions but extra fuel capacity and entered service with KLM in 1971.

BOEING 757

Country of Origin: USA

Production: Number ordered 162; in airline service 102 (60)

Power Plant: Two Rolls-Royce RB 211-535C turbofans each rated at 16,980kgp (37,400lb st)

Performance: Cruising speed 899km/h (540mph) at 10,670m (35,000ft); range with max payload about 2,000km (1,250mls)

Weights: Typical operating weight empty 61,290kg (135,000lb); max take-off weight 99,880kg (220,000lb); max zero fuel weight 83,536kg (184,000lb); max landing weight 89,892kg (198,000lb)

Dimensions: Span 37.95m (124ft 6in); overall length 47.32m (155ft 3in); overall height 13.56m (44ft 6in); wing area 181.25m² (1,951sq ft)

Seating Capacity: 186

History: Designed as a replacement for the 727, the 757 has kept the same fuselage width but incorporates a completely new wing and new Rolls-Royce RB 211 engines for which the British government supplied the development finance. British Airways initially ordered 19 of what are reputed to be the world's most fuel-efficient aircraft. The 757 made its first flight on February 1982 and entered service in December of the same year.

BOEING 767

Country of Origin: USA

Production: Number ordered 193; in airline service 122 (72)

Power Plant: Two Pratt & Whitney JT9D-7R4A turbofans each rated at 20,112kgp (44,300lb st) for take-off; fuel capacity approximately 41,640lit (11,000 US gal)

Performance: Cruising speed Mach 0.80 at 11,887m (39,000ft); design range 3,700km (2,300mls)

Weights: Operating weight empty 78,397kg (172,680lb); max payload 27,694kg (61,000lb); max take-off weight 128,030kg (282,000lb); max zero fuel weight 109,870kg (242,000lb); max landing weight 116,680kg (257,000lb)

Dimensions: Span 47.24m (155ft 0in); length 48.46m (159ft 00in); overall height 15.38m (50ft 5in)

Seating Capacity: 200

History: With a production rate of only 2 per month, the future of the all-new Boeing twin-jet, which utilises advanced aluminium light-weight alloys, looks assured for the immediate future. The 767 also embodies the use of light-weight compounds of graphite epoxy-bonded particles which offer improved stress and anti-corrosion benefits. First orders were placed by United Airlines and the first flight took place in September 1981, with airline service commencing in August 1982.

BRISTOL 175 BRITANNIA Srs310

Country of Origin: United Kingdom
Production: Number built 100; number in airline service 9

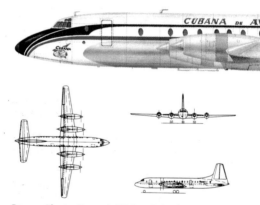

Power Plant: Four 4,450shp Bristol Proteus 765 turboprops
Performance: Max cruising speed 639km/h (397mph); best economy cruise 575km/h (357mph); range with max payload 4,990km (3,100mls); range with max fuel 5,327km (3,310mls)

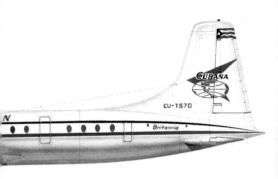

Weights: Empty equipped 42,410kg (93,500lb); max payload 15,650kg (34,500ib); max take-off 83,915kg (185,000lb)

Dimensions: Span 43.36m (142ft 3in); length 37.87m (124ft 3in); height 11.43m (37ft 6in); wing area 192.76m² (2,074sq ft)

Seating Capacity: Up to 139

History: The aircraft was first flown on 16 August 1952 as the Srs 100. The Srs 300 made its first flight on 31 December 1956. It had a stretched fuselage and up-rated Proteus engines. BOAC were the largest purchaser of the 300, which was designated 310, the last two digits being the airline coding. The RAF also took delivery of 23 aircraft, which they subsequently sold off in 1975.

BRITISH AEROSPACE ATP

Country of Origin: United Kingdom
Production: Number ordered 7; in airline service 0 (7)
Power Plant: Two 2,520ehp Pratt & Whitney PW124/125 turboprops

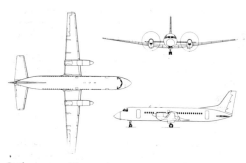

Performance: Max cruise speed 492km/h (266kt) at 4,672m (15,000ft); range with max payload 1,576km (851nm); range with max fuel 4,386km (2,368nm)

Weights: Ramp weight 22,589kg (49,800lb); max take-off weight 22,453kg (49,500lb); max landing weight 21,773kg (48,000lb); operating weight empty 13,595kg (29,970lb)

Dimensions: Span 30.63m (100ft 5in); length 26.01m (85ft 5in); height 7.14m (32ft 4in); wing area 71.3m² (843sq ft)

Seating Capacity: 64

History: A stretched development of the BAe748, the Advanced Turboprop received its go-ahead in March 1984. Its first flight was on 6 August 1986 and orders have already been received from British Midland and Liat. There is also a possibility that the ATP could be manufactured under license in the Soviet Union where Aeroflot would use it to replace the ageing IL-14 and IL-24s.

BRITISH AEROSPACE HS 125 Srs 700

Country of Origin: United Kingdom
Production: Number ordered 623 all versions
Power Plant: Two Garrett AiResearch TFE731-3-1H turbofans each rated at 1,680kgp (3,700lb st) for take-off
Performance: Max speed 592km/h (368mph) at sea

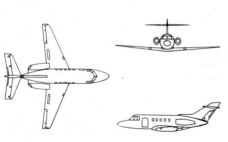

level; service ceiling 12,500m (41,000ft); range with max payload 3,556km (2,210mls)

Weights: Empty operating 5,747kg (12,670lb); max payload 1,068kg (2,355lb); max take-off 10,977kg (24,200lb); max landing 9,979kg (22,000lb)

Dimensions: Span 14.33m (47ft 0in); length 15.46m (50ft 8.5m); height 5.36m (17ft 7in); wing area 32.8m² (353sq ft)

Seating Capacity: 8

History: Originating with de Havilland, the prototype DH125 first flew on 13 August 1962. The first DH125 production craft were designated Srs10 and were powered by Viper 520 engines. The prototype Srs 700 first flew on 28 June 1976 powered by TFE 731 engines. The Srs 800 followed, powered by TFE 731-5 turbofans, the fuselage slightly lengthened and the wing span increased by 1.32m (4ft 4in) and a gross weight increased by 909kg (2000lb).

BRITISH AEROSPACE JETSTREAM 31

Country of Origin: United Kingdom
Production: Number ordered 123
Power Plant: Two 940shp Garrett TPE-10 turboprops
Performance: Max speed 210km/h (113kt); max cruise

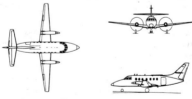

speed 486km/h (263kt) at 4,572m (15,000ft); range
with max payload 1,519km (820nm); range with max
fuel 2,240km (1,391mls)

Weights: Max take-off 6,950kg (15,322lb); max landing 6,600kg (14,500lb); empty operating 4,360kg (9,613lb)
Dimensions: Span 15.85m (52ft 0in); length 14.36m (47ft 3in); height 5.32m (17ft 4.5in); wing area 25.2m² (271sq ft)
Seating Capacity: 18
History: Originally the Handley Page Jetstream, which first flew on 18 August 1967 and entered service in 1969. Handley Page collapsed in 1970 after delivering only 38, with 10 more in production. In 1978 British Aerospace, who had acquired the manufacturing rights, relaunched the Jetstream with deliveries commencing in 1981. Production is now running at 4 per month and BAe is considering launching a stretched version to carry between 24 and 27 passengers.

BRITISH AEROSPACE TRIDENT 2E

Country of Origin: United Kingdom
Production: Number built 117; in airline service 44

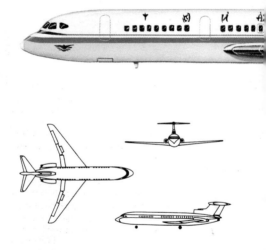

Power Plant: Three 5,425kg (11,960lb) thrust Rolls-Royce RB163-25 MK 512-5W Spey turbofans
Performance: Cruising speed 974km/h (605mph) at 7,620m (25,000ft); economic cruising speed 959km/h

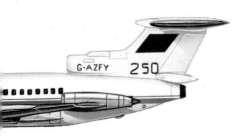

(596mph) at 9,145m (30,000ft); range with typical payload and fuel reserves 3,965km (2,464mls)

Weights: Empty operating 33,203kg (73,200lb); max take-off 65,317kg (144,000lb)

Dimensions: Span 29.87m (98ft 0in); length 34.98m (114ft 9in); height 8.23m (27ft 0in); wing area 135.26m² (1,456.0sq ft)

Seating Capacity: 139

History: The Trident 1 first entered service as a short/medium-haul airliner on 1 April 1964. No prototypes were built and it was BEA's first jet passenger airliner. The Trident 2E, with wing span increased by 2.49m (8ft 2in), flew on 27 July 1967 and entered service with BEA on 18 April 1968. A further variant, the 3B with stretched fuselage, 5m (16ft 5in) longer to accommodate up to 180 passengers, first flew on 11 December 1969 and incorporated a 'booster' engine in the tail above the fuselage to improve take-off performance. The Trident 3 entered service with BEA on April 1971.

BRITISH AEROSPACE 810 VISCOUNT
Country of Origin: United Kingdom
Production: Number built 440; in airline service 44
Power Plant: Four 2,100ehp Rolls-Royce Dart 525 turboprops.

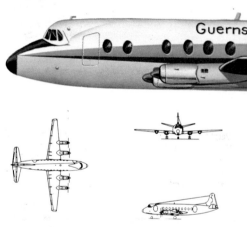

Performance: Cruising speed, 563km/h (350mph) at 6100m (20,000ft), max payload range 27757kg (1,725mls); max fuel range 2,830km (1,760mls).

Weights: Basic operating 18,753kg (41,565lb); max take-off 32,886kg (72,500lb); max payload 6,577kb (14,500lb).

Dimensions: Span 28.5m (93ft 8in); length 26.11m (85ft 8in); wing area 89.46m² (963sq ft).

Seating Capacity: 65

History: The Vickers Viscount was the world's first turboprop transport, entering service with BEA on 18 April 1953 between London and Cyprus with a seating capacity of 47. The type 810 was the final variation, utilizing more powerful engines. It first flew in December 1957. The last 6 aircraft to be built in 1964 were for CAAC of China and represented CAAC's first purchase of Western aircraft.

BRITISH AEROSPACE ONE-ELEVEN 500

Country of Origin: United Kingdom
Production: Number built 230; in airline service 162
Power Plant: Two 5,693kg (12,550lb) thrust Rolls-

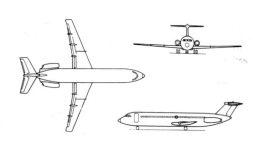

Royce Spey MK 512 DW turbofans
Performance: Max cruising speed 871km/h (541mph) at 6,400m (21,000ft); max cruising height 10,670m

(35,000ft); range with fuel reserves and full payload 2,726km (1,694mls)

Weights: Empty operating 24,386kg (53,762lb); max take-off 47,400kg (104,500lb)

Dimensions: Span 28.50m (93ft 6in); length 32.61m 107ft 0in); height 7.47m (24ft 6in); wing area 95.78m² (1,031.0sq ft)

Seating Capacity: 119

History: Originally designed by Hunting Aircraft Ltd as a four-abreast 48-seat airliner, with a 1,610km (1,000mls) range, the One-Eleven (as it became known after Hunting were taken over by BAC) first flew on 20 August 1963 and the series 200 aircraft entered service on 9 April 1965. Variants include the Series 300, first ordered by American Airlines and altered to meet US regulations, and the Series 500 which appeared in 1966 with a stretched fuselage, increased by 4.11m (13ft 6in), and wing span increased by 1.2m (5ft).

BRITISH AEROSPACE BAe146 Srs 100

Country of Origin: United Kingdom
Production: Number ordered 61; in airline service 32
(25)
Power Plant: Four Arco Lyconing ALF502R-3 tubofans

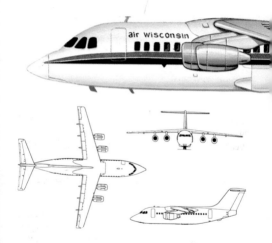

rated at 3,040kgp (6,700lb st) for take-off; fuel capacity 11,450lit (2,540gal)
Performance: Max operating speed Mach 0.70; eco-

nomic cruising speed 708km/h (440mph) at 9,145m
(130,000ft); range with fuel reserves and max payload
797km (495mls)

Weights: Empty operating 21,319kg (47,000lb); max
take-off 37,308kg (82,250lb)

Dimensions: Span 36.34m (86ft 5in); length 26.16m
(85ft 10in); height 8.61m (28ft 3in); wing area 77.29m²
(832.0sq ft)

Seating Capacity: 93

History: Designed as a short-haul/feeder aircraft
aimed at smaller airlines, the BAe146 boasts excellent
ease of operation, good economies and efficient
product at a sales price of about $15m. First flight was
in September 1981, and first flight of the Series 200
with additional seating capacity of up to 109 was in
August 1982.

BRITISH AEROSPACE BAe748 Srs 2B

Country of Origin: United Kingdom
Production: Number ordered 377; in airline service 161
Power Plant: Two 1,700ekw (2,280eshp) Rolls-Royce Dart RDa7 mh 536-2 turboprops
Performance: Cruising speed, at weight of 17,237kg

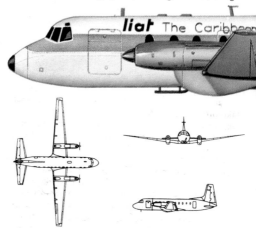

(38,000lb), 452km/h (281mph); service ceiling 7,620m (25,000ft); range with max payload and fuel reserves 1,455km (904mls)

Weights: Empty operating 12,206kg (26,910lb); max take-off 21,092kg (46,500lb)

Dimensions: Span 31.23m (102ft 5.5in); length 20.42m (67ft 0in); height 7.57m (24ft 10in); wing area 77.0m² (828.87sq ft)

Seating Capacity: 58

History: First prototype flew on 24 June 1960 and a second on 10 April 1961. The first production model flew on 30 August 1961 and entered service with Skyways Coach-Air the following year. The Srs 2 with uprated engines first flew (as a converted Srs 1) on 6 November 1961 and entered service with BKS Air Transport the following year. A much improved version, the Srs 2B, with wing span increased by 1.22m (4ft), first flew on 22 June 1977.

BRITTEN-NORMAN ISLANDER BN-2A-2

Country of Origin: United Kingdom
Production: Number built 1,070
Power Plant: Two 260hp Avro Lycoming 0-540-E4C5 piston engines
Performance: Max speed 290km/h (180mph); typical cruise 270km/h (168mph) at 2750m (9,000ft); initial rate of climb 6.35m/sec (1,250ft/min); service ceiling

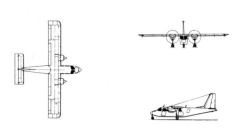

5,013m (10,400ft); range at typical speed 1,287km (800mls)

Weights: Basic operating 1,695kg (3,738lb); max take-off 2,857kg (6,300lb)

Dimensions: Span 14.94m (49ft 0in); length 10.86m (35ft 7.75in); height 4.18m (13ft 8.75in); wing area 30.19m² (325sq ft)

Seating Capacity: 9

History: The first prototype flew on 13 June 1965, a second on 17 December 1965 and a third on 20 August 1966, following which production was put in hand and the first production craft flew on 24 April 1967. The Islander entered service on 13 August 1967 with Glosair and two days later with Loganair.

BRITTEN-NORMAN TRISLANDER

Country of Origin: United Kingdom
Power Plant: Three 260 Lycoming 0-540-E4C5 piston engines
Performance: Max speed 294km/h (183mph) at sea level; max cruising speed 283km/h (176mph) at 1,988m (6,500ft); typical cruise 280km/h (174mph) at 2,750m (9,000ft); initial rate of climb 4.98m/sec (980ft/

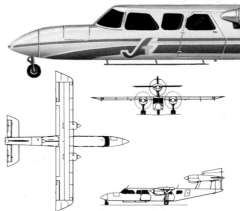

min); service ceiling 4010m (13,150ft); range with max payload 338km (210mls); range with max fuel 1,384km (860mls)
Weight: Basic operating 2,800kg (6,178lb); max

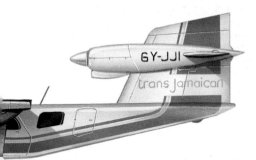

payload 1,610kg (3,550lb); max take-off 4,536kg (10,000lb)

Dimensions: Span 16.15m (53ft 0in); length 13.34m (43ft 9in); length with extended nose 14.48m (47ft 6in); height 4.11m (13ft 5.75in); wing area 31.25m² (337sq ft)

Seating Capacity: 18

History: An evolution from the Islander, the Trislander has considerable commonality including the fuselage cross section, mainplane and power plant. Differences include the stretched fuselage and a third engine which is located in the tail fin. First prototype flight was on 11 September 1970 and first production model on 6 March 1971, with deliveries starting on 29 June 1971. The first flight of the Trislander with the stretched fuselage was on 18 August 1974.

CANADAIR CL-44D-4

Country of Origin: Canada
Production: Number built 39; in airline service 12
Power Plant: Four 5,730hp Rolls-Royce Type 515/10 turboprops
Performance: Cruising speed 612km/h (386mph) at

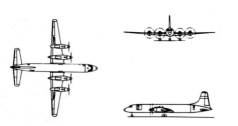

6,100m (20,000ft) at a weight of 86,180kg (190,000lb); range with max payload 5,245km (3,260mls); range with max fuel 8,990km (5,587mls) with payload of 16,132kg (35,564lb)

Weights: Operating weight empty 40,348kg (88,952lb); max payload 28,725kg (63,272lb); max take-off 95,250kg (210,000lb); max landing 74,843kg (160,000lb)

Dimensions: Span 43.37m (142ft 3.5in); length 41.73m (136ft 10.75in); height 11.80m (38ft 8in); wing area 192.76m² (2,075sq ft)

Seating Capacity: 178

History: First flown on 15 November 1959, the first 12 production models designated CL-44D were for the RCAF. The CL-44D-4 was the first production aircraft to feature a hinged tail unit and rear fuselage which allowed straight-in loading of large pallets. The prototype CL-44D-4 first flew on 16 November 1960 and first deliveries were to Flying Tiger on May 1961. Flying Tiger, Seaboard and Slick all operated scheduled cargo flights, whilst Loftleider of Iceland used a 178-seat passenger version on transatlantic flights.

CANADAIR CHALLENGER
Country of Origin: Canada

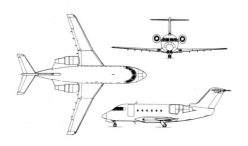

Power Plant: Two Avco Lycoming ALF 502L turbofans each rated at 3,405kgp (7,500lb st)

Performance: Max cruising speed 488km/h (561mph) above 10,980m (36,000ft); max ratified ceiling 14,935m (47,000ft); max range 6,667km (4,143mls)

Weights: Operating empty 9,172kg (20,220lb); max payload, with max fuel, 427kg (940lb); max take-off 16,329kg (36,000ft); max landing 14,970kg (33,000lb)

Dimensions: Span 18.84m (61ft 10in); length 20.85m (68ft 5in); height 6.30m (20ft 8in); wing area 41.81m² (450sq ft)

Seating Capacity: 28

History: Originally designated the LearStar 600, the production and marketing rights were acquired by Canadair Ltd in 1976. THe only major design alteration was to switch to a 'T'-tail. The first flight was on 8 November 1978.

CASA 212 AVIOCAR

Country of Origin: Spain
Production: Number produced 389
Power Plant: Two 776ehp Garrett-AiResearch TPE331-5-251C turboprops
Performance: Max speed 370km/h (230mph) at 3,660m (12,000ft); cruising speed 315km/h (196mph) at 3,660m (12,000ft); rate of climb 9.1m/sec (1,800ft/min); service ceiling 8,140m (26,000ft); range 480km (300mls) with max payload

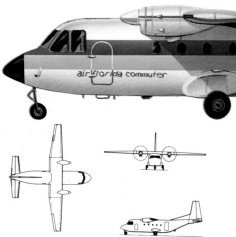

Weights: Empty equipped 3,905kg (8,690lb); max payload 2,000kg (4,410lb); max take-off weight 6,500kg (14,330lb)

Dimensions: Span 19.0m (62ft 4in); length 15.20m (49ft 10.5in); height 6.30m (20ft 8in); wing area 40.0m² (430.6sq ft)

Seating Capacity: 19

History: First prototype flight was on 26 March 1971; the C-212-100 was initially put into production for the Spanish Air Force and the first production model flew on 17 November 1972. The C-212 series had more powerful engines than the original TPE 331-10R.

CASA-NUSANTARA AIRTECH CN-235

Country of Origin: Spain/Indonesia

Production: Number ordered 130; in airline service nil (66)

Power Plant: Two 1,700shp GE CT7-7A turboprops

Performance: Max speed 174km/h (94kt); max cruise speed 446km/h (241kt) at 5,486m (18,000ft); range with max payload 842km (523mls); range with max fuel 4,824km

Weights: Ramp 14,450kg (31,857lb); max take-off

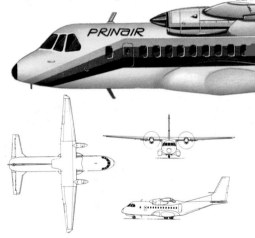

14,400kg (31,747lb); max landing 14,200kg (31,306lb); empty 9,400kg (20,723lb)

Dimensions: Span 25.8m (84ft 6in); length 21.35m (70ft); height 8.17m (26ft 8in); wing area 59.1m² (636sq ft)

Seating Capacity: 44

History: A joint venture between Spain and Indonesia following the success of the CASA 212-300 which Nusantara (formerly Nurtanio) assembled under license, the CN-235 is unfortunately more than a year behind schedule due to control ineffectiveness in the horizontal stabilizer. Meanwhile orders continue to mount with a further 23 options on top of the 130 announced sales.

CESSNA CITATION 1

Country of Origin: USA

Power Plant: Two Pratt & Whitney (Canada) JT15D-1A turbofans each rated at 998kgp (2,200lb st) for take-off

Performance: Max cruising speed 650km/h (404mph); initial rate of climb 13.6m/sec (2,680ft/min); max

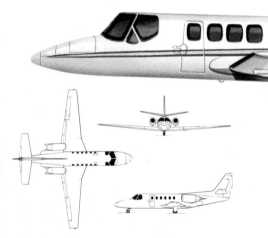

operating altitude 12,505m (41,000ft); max range 2,470km (1,535mls)

Weights: Empty operating 2,935kg (6,464lb): max

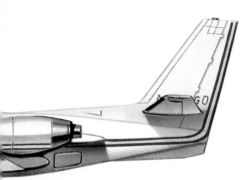

take-off 5,834kg (12,850lb); max landing 5,153kg (11,350lb)

Dimensions: Span 14.36m (47ft 1in); length 13.27m (43ft 6in); height 4.37ft 4in)

Seating Capacity: 8

History: Launched as the Fanjet 500 by Cessna in October 1968 as a purely business jet, the first prototype flew on 15 September 1969. The name was altered to Model 500 Citation before the second prototype flew on 23 January 1970. Deliveries commenced in September 1971. The model 501 Citation 1 incorporated uprated engines and the wing span increased by 2.21m (7ft 3in) and entered service in 1977. The Cessna Citation 11 with stretched fuselage and uprated engines was introduced in February 1978 with a seating capacity of 10.

CESSNA 404 TITAN

Country of Origin: USA
Production: Number built 395
Power Plant: Two Continental G7510-520M flat- six piston engines each rated at 375hp for take-off
Performance: Max speed 363km/h (225mph) at sea level and 433km/h (269mph) at 4877m (16,000ft); max

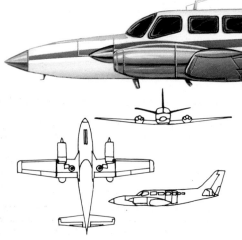

cruising speed 359km (223mph) at 3050m (10,000ft); initial rate of climb 7.7m/sec (1,515ft/min); service

ceiling 6767m (22,200ft); range with max payload 1641km (1020mls)

Weights: Empty operating 2,156kg (4,757lb); max take-off 3,705kg (8,300lb); max landing 3,674kg (8,100lb)

Dimensions: Span 14.02m (46ft 0in); length 12.04m (39ft 5in); height 3.99m (13ft 1in); wing area 22.48m² (242sq ft)

Seating Capacity: 6-8

History: The Titan first flew in prototype form on 26 February 1975 and was offered to both business and third-level commuter airlines. Deliveries began in October 1976 at a production rate of 5 per month but production ceased in 1982.

CESSNA 402 UTILINER

Country of Origin: USA
Production: Number built 1,536
Power Plant: Two Continental TS10-520-E flat- six piston engines each rated at 300hp for take-off

Performance: Max speed 420km/h (261mph) at 4,875m (16,000ft); max cruising speed 386km/h (240mph) at

6,100m (20,000ft); initial rate of climb 8.2m/sec (1,610ft/min); service ceiling 7,980m (26,180ft); range 1,860-2,280km (1,156-1,417mls)

Weights: Empty operating 1,767kg (3,896lb); max take-off 2,857kg (6,300lb); max landing 2,812kg (6,200lb)

Dimensions: Span 12.15 m (39ft 10in); length 11.5m (36ft 1in); height 3.56m (11ft 8in); wing area 18.18m² (195.7sq ft)

Seating Capacity: 10

History: The Cessna 411 was first flown on 18 July 1962. Over 300 were built by 1968, when the 411 was replaced by the lighter Cessna 401. The 401, with accommodation for 8, first flew on 25 August 1965. The 402 was introduced alongside the 401, which gave way in 1971 to the 402B.

CONVAIR CV-440 METROPOLITAN

Country of Origin: USA
Production: Number built 181; in airline service 31
Power Plant: Two 2,500hp Pratt & Whitney R-2800-CB16 or -CB17 piston radials
Performance: Max cruising speed 483km/h (300mph) at 3,962m (13,000ft); best economy cruise 465km/h

(289mph) at 6,100m (20,000ft); initial rate of climb 6.4m/sec (1,260ft/min); service ceiling 7,590m (24,900ft); range with max payload 459km (285mls); range with max fuel 3,106 (1,930mls)

N478KW

Weights: Basic operating 15,110kg (33,314lb); max payload 5,820kg (12,836lb); max take-off 22,544kg (49,700lb)

Dimensions: Span 32.12m (105ft 4in); length 24.84m (81ft 6in); height 8.59m (28ft 2in); wing area 85.5m² (920sq ft)

Seating Capacity: 52

History: The Metropolitan was instigated by AA as a post-war replacement for the Douglas DC-3; their first order was for 75 of the model 240. The 340 entered service on 28 March 1952. The prototype Convair Model 440 Metropolitan flew on 6 October 1955. A more refined and comfortable airliner, it entered service with Continental Airlines in early 1956. The fuselage of the 440 was another 0.7m (2ft 4in) longer than the 340 R.

CONVAIR CV-580

Country of Origin: USA

Production: Number converted 175; in airline service 95

Power Plant: Two 3,750shp Allison 501-013H turboprops

Performance: Cruising speed 550km/h (342mph);

range with max fuel 4,611km (2,866mls)

Weights: Max payload 4,023kg (8,870lb); max take-off 26,371kg (58,140lb)

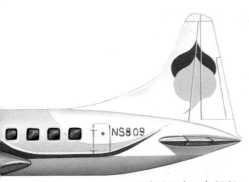

Dimensions: Span 32.12m (105ft 4in); length 24.84m (81ft 6in); height 8.89m (29ft 2in); wing area 85.5m² (920sq ft)

Seating Capacity: 40

History: A large-scale conversion programme to convert piston-radial-engined Convair 240/340/440's to turboprop engines began in 1954 by D. Napier & Son Ltd, using Eland NE1.1 turboprops. The first conversion flew in February 1955, followed by a further six which entered service with Allegheny Airlines in July 1959, and which were designated Convair 540's. These conversions were followed by the Allison-Convair or Super Convair using Allison 501-D13 turboprops, which was designated the Convair 580. They entered airline service with Frontier in mid 1964 having made their first flight on 19 January 1960.

CONVAIR CV-640

Country of Origin: USA
Production: Number converted 68; in airline service 39

Power Plant: Two 3,025eshp Rolls-Royce Dart 542-4 turboprops
Performance: Cruising speed 482km/h (300mph); range with max payload 1,975km (1,230mls) at 4,575m (15,000ft); range with max fuel 3,138km (1,950mls) at 4,575m (15,000ft)

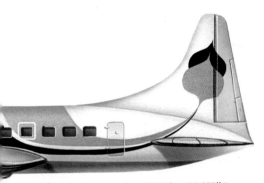

Weights: Basic operating 13,732kg (30,275lb); max payload 7,167kg (15,800lb); max take-off 24,950kg (55,000lb) or 25,855kg (57,000lb) if Model 440 with outer wing fuel and fuel dumping

Dimensions: Span 32.12m (105ft 4in); length 24.84m (81ft 6in); height 8.59m (28ft 2in); wing area 85.5m² (920sq ft)

Seating Capacity: 44-52

History: Entering service on 22 December 1965 with Caribair, the 28 Convair 640s represented the last of the conversions of the Convair 340s and 440s to turboprops. Using Rolls-Royce Dart 542 engines, Convair became involved in conversion for the first time, offering either kits or converted airframes. Other airlines to place orders were Hawaiian and Air Algerie.

CURTISS C-46 COMMANDO

Country of Origin: USA
Production: Number built 2,882; in airline service 31
Power Plant: Two 2,000shp Pratt & Whitney R-2800-34 piston engines

AIR HAITI

Performance: Max speed 433km/h (269mph); max cruising speed 301km/h (187mph) at 2,133m (7,000ft);

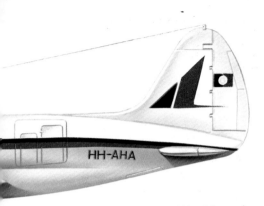

HH-AHA

initial rate of climb 6.6m/sec (1,300ft.min); service ceiling 8,412m (27,600ft); range with max payload 117km (110mls); range with max fuel 1,880km (1,170mls) with 2,585kg (5,700lb) payload

Weights: Empty equipped 14,970kg (33,000lb); max payload 5,265kg (11,630lb); max take-off (passenger) 21,364kg (47,100lb), (freighter) 21,772kg (48,000lb)

Dimensions: Span 32.92m (108ft 0in); length 23,27m (76ft 4in); height 6.60m (21ft 8in); wing area 126m² (1,358sq ft)

Seating Capacity: 50

History: Launched in 1938 to compete with the Douglas DC-3, the first prototype flight was made on 26 March 1940.

DASSAULT-BREGUET FALCON 20
Country of Origin: France

Production: 500 plus
Power Plant: Two General Electric CF700-2D-2 turbofans each rated at 1,960kgp (4,315lb st) for take-off
Performance: Max cruising speed 862km/h (536mph)

at 7,620m (25,000ft); max range 3,570km (2,230mls)
Weights: Empty operating 7,240kg (1,5970lb); max payload 1,500kg (3.320lb); max take-off weight 13,000kg (28,660lb)
Dimensions: Span 16.3m (53ft 6in); length 17.15m (56ft 3in); height 5.32m (17ft 5in); wing area 41.00m² (440sq ft)
Seating Capacity: 12
History: The Falcon 20 was Dassault-Breguet's first business jet. The prototype first flew on 4 May 1963 and the Falcon 20 or Mystere XX, as it is known in France, entered service in June 1965. The aircraft has proved to be very successful, with many variants being produced, prior to the introduction of the scaled-down Falcon 10 aircraft, which entered service in 1973.

DASSAULT BREGUET MERCURE 100

Country of Origin: France
Production: Number built 11; in airline service 11
Power Plant: Two 7,030kgp (15,500lb st) Pratt &
Whitney JT8D-15 turbofans
Performance: Max cruising speed 932km/h (579mph)
at 6,100m (20,000ft); best economy cruise 858km/h

(533mph) at 9,145m (30,000ft); initial rate of climb
16.76m/sec (3,300ft.min) at 45,359kg (100,000lb)
weight; range with max payload 750km (466mls);

range with max fuel 1,650km (1,025mls)

Weights: Basic operating 31,800kg (70,107lb); max payload 16,200kg (35,715lb); max take-off 56,500kg (124,560lb)

Dimensions: Span 30.55m (100ft 3in); length 34.84m (114ft 3.5in); height 11.36m (37ft 3.25in); wing area 116.0m² (1,249sq ft)

Seating Capacity: 155

History: First flown with JR8D-11 engines on 28 May 1971. The production aircraft entered service with Air Inter on 4 June 1974 with JT8D-15 turbofans. Financed largely by the French government and European Airlines, Dassault only contributed 14 per cent to the development costs, although budgets were based on initial orders for 50 aircraft. The internal French airline, Air Inter, remains the only operator.

DE HAVILLAND CANADA DHC-6 TWIN OTTER Srs300

Country of Origin: Canada
Power Plant: Two 486-ekw (652eshp) Pratt & Whitney
Aircraft of Canada PT6A-27 turboprops
Performance: Max cruising speed 338km/h (210mph)
at 3,050m (10,000ft); service ceiling 8,140m (26,700ft);

range with 1,134kg (2,500lb) payload 1,297km (806mls)

Weights: Empty operating 3,363kg (7,415lb); max take-off 5,670kg (12,500lb)

Dimensions: Span 19.81m (65ft 0in); length 15.77m (51ft 9in); height 5.94m (19ft 6in); wing area 39.02m² (420.0sq ft)

Seating Capacity: 20

History: Production of the first five twin-engined STOL aircraft began in November 1964 and, because of the large commonality with the single-engined Otter de Havilland were able to make a first flight on 20 May 1965. In Spring 1969 deliveries of the Srs 300 began.

DE HAVILLAND CANADA DASH 7

Country of Origin: Canada
Production: Number ordered 103; in airline service 94
Power Plant: Four 1,120shp Pratt & Whitney (VACL) PT6A-50 turboprops
Performance: Max cruising speed 452km/h (281mph) at 4,570m (15,000ft); initial rate of climb 6.51m/sec (1,310ft/min); service ceiling 6,770m (22,200ft); range

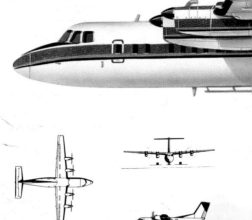

with max payload 1,504km (935mls); range with max fuel 2,293km (1,425mls)

Weights: Operating empty 11,730kg (25,860lb); max payload 5,280kg (11,640lb): max take-off 19,504kg (43,000lb)

Dimensions: Span 28.35m (93ft 0in); length 24.50m (80ft 4in); height 8.00m (26ft 3in); wing area 79.9m² (860sq ft)

Seating Capacity: 48-54

History: First flown in prototype form on 27 March 1974 and as a production model on 30 May 1977, the De Havilland Dash 7 entered service with Rocky Mountain Airways on 3 February 1978. The Dash 7 is a STOL aircraft designated to utilize runways as short as 610m (2,000ft).

DE HAVILLAND CANADA DASH 8

Country of Origin: Canada
Production: Number ordered 82; in airline service 19 (63)
Power Plant: Two 1,342kw (1,800shp) Pratt & Whitney Aircraft of Canada PW120 turboprops
Performance: Max cruising speed 499km/h (310mph)

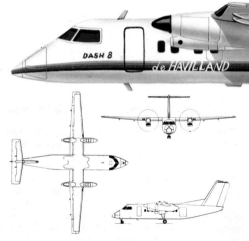

at 4,570m (15,000ft); normal range with fuel reserves 1,056km (656mls)

Weights: Empty operating 9,793kg (21,590lb); max take-off 14,969kg (33,000lb)

Dimensions: Span 25.90m (84ft 11.5in); length 22.25m (73ft 0in); height 7.44m (24ft 5in); wing area 54.35m² (585.0sq ft)

Seating Capacity: 36

History: First flown in June 1983, the Dash 8 entered service with NorOntair in October 1984. Already sold to 20 customers at a price of about $5.5m, De Havilland Canada are increasing production from 3 to 4 aircraft a month. A stretched 300 series has already been launched with a seating capacity for up to 50 passengers. First deliveries of these are scheduled for spring 1988.

DOUGLAS DC-3

Country of Origin: USA
Production: Number built 10,926; in airline service 353

Power Plant: Two 1,200hp Pratt & Whitney R-1830-92 Twin Wasp piston engines
Performance: Max speed 346km/h (215mph); high speed cruise 312km/h (194mph); economical cruise 266km/h (165mph) at 1829m (6,000ft); initial climb

4.5m/sec (1,070ft/min); service ceiling 6,675m (21,900ft); range with max payload 563km (350mls); range with max fuel 2,430km (1,510mls)

Weights: Operating weight empty 8,030kg (17,720lb); max payload 3,000kg (6,600lb); max take-off 11,430kg (25,200lb)

Dimensions: Span 28.96m (95ft 0in); length 19.66m (64ft 6in); height 5.16m (16ft 11.5in); wing area 91.7m² (987sq ft)

Seating Capacity: 24

History: The most widely used and possibly the most famous of all airliners, the Douglas Commercial 3 has been flying for over 50 years, having entered service with American Airlines between New York and Chicago on 25 June 1936. Initially powered by 920hp Wright GR-1820-95 cyclone engines.

DORNIER Do228-201
Country of Origin: West Germany
Production: Number built 120; in airline service 100
Power Plant: Two 715shp Garrett 7PE 331-5 turboprops
Performance: Max speed 148km/h (80kt); max cruise

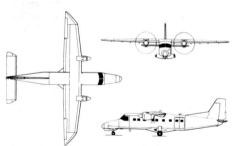

speed 424km/h (231kt) at 3,048m (10,000ft); range with max payload 1,112km (600nm); range with max fuel 1,390km (750nm)

Weights: Max take-off 5,980kg (13,183lb); max landing 5,700kg (12,676lb); empty operating 3,557kg (7,842lb)

Dimensions: Span 16.97m (55ft 8in); length 16.65m (54ft 4in); height 4.86m (15ft 8in); wing area 32m² (344sq ft)

Seating Capacity: 19

History: A most distinctive aircraft with its drooped nose, tapered wingtips and a slope-sided fuselage, the 228 is also produced under license in India by Hindustan Aeronautics, whose first production craft flew in February 1986 just prior to the 100th delivery from West Germany. An excellent airfield performance has meant that the 228 is taking over from the ageing Twin Otter as the 'difficult conditions' workhorse. The initial 100 series was a shorter 15-seat variant.

DOUGLAS DC-4

Country of Origin: USA
Production: Number built 1,242; in airline service 21
Power Plant: Four 1,450hp Pratt & Whitney R-2,000-25D-13G Twin Wasp piston radial engines

Performance: Max speed 426km/h (265mph); cruising speed 33km/h (207mph) at 3,050m (10,000ft) at 29,484kg (65,000lb) mean weight; service ceiling 5,791m (19,000ft); range with max payload 1,850km (1,150mls); range with max fuel 3,510km (2,180mls)

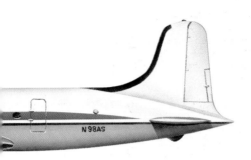

Weights: Empty equipped 20,865kg (46,000lb); max payload 6,440kg (14,200lb); max take-off weight 33,112kg (73,000lb); max landing and max zero fuel weight 28,80kg (63,500lb)

Dimensions: Span 35.82m (117ft 6in); length 28.47m (93ft 5in); height 8.41m (27ft 7in); wing area 135.8m² (1,462sq ft)

Seating Capacity: 42

History: Due to the intervention of World War II, the production lines at Douglas were taken over by the military so that when the first DC-4A production aircraft flew on 14 February 1942, it was in the form of a military C-54 Skymaster. More than 1,000 military craft were built prior to American Overseas Airlines taking delivery in late 1945. The DC-4s offered excellent economy and were therefore eagerly purchased from the military as they became available in 1946.

DOUGLAS DC-6B

Country of Origin: USA

Production: Number built, all DC-6 variants, 537; of DC-6B 288 were built; in airline service 68

Power Plant: Four 2,500hp Pratt & Whitney R-2800-

CB17 piston radial engines

Performance: Cruising speed 509km/h (316mph); initial rate of climb 6.2m/sec (1,120ft/min); range with max payload 4,828km (3,000mls); range with max fuel 7,596km (4,720mls)

Weights: Basic operating 26,595kg (58,635lb); max payload 11,143kg (24,565lb); max take-off 48,534kg

(107,000lb)

Dimensions: Span 35.81m (117ft 6in); length 32.2m (105ft 7in); height 8.92m (29ft 3in); wing area 135.9m² (1,463sq ft)

Seating Capacity: Basic 52

History: The first commercial order for 50 DC-6 aircraft was placed by American Airlines in 1944, with further orders from United soon after. The first production DC-6 flew in June 1946 and deliveries to both American and United commenced in November 1946, with the first commercial service being flown on 27 April 1947. Scheduled flying time coast-to-coast eastbound was 10 hours, and 11 hours westbound. The DC-6A, with lengthened fuselage, entered production in 1948, and the DC-6B made its first flight on 2 February 1951. The DC-6B was one of the best piston-engined airliners, having outstanding mechanical reliability, and it saw service with many of the world's leading airlines.

139

DOUGLAS DC-7C

Country of Origin: USA

Production: Number built of all DC-7s 338; of DC-7Cs 121 were built; number in airline service 4

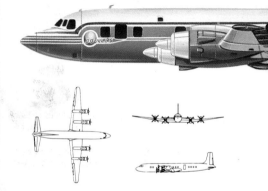

Power Plant: Four 3,400hp Wright R3350-EA1 or EA4 piston radial engines

Performance: Cruising speed 555km/h (345mph); service ceiling 6,615m (21,700ft); range with max payload 5,810km (3,610mls); range with max fuel 9,077km (5,642mls)

Weights: Basic operating 36,287kg (80,000lb); max payload 9,752kg (21,500lb); max take-off 64,865kg (143,000lb)

Dimensions: Span 38.8m (127ft 6in); length 34.23m (112ft 3in); height 9.65m (31ft 8in); wing area 152.0m² (1,637sq ft)

Seating Capacity: 105

History: The first DC-7 flight was made on 18 May 1953, the final development, and the last piston-engined commercial aircraft to be built by Douglas, was the DC-7C. It entered service with Pan American on 1 June 1956, and 12 other airlines including BOAC also placed orders. SAS flew the first 'over-the-pole' Europe-Far East service on 24 February 1957.

DOUGLAS DC-8 Srs 50

Country of Origin: USA

Production: Number built 556; in airline service 258

Power Plant: Four 7,945kgp (17,000lb st) Pratt & Whitney JT3D-1 or 8,172kgp (18,000lb st) JT3D-3 or 3B turbofans

Performance: Max cruising speed 933km/h (580mph);

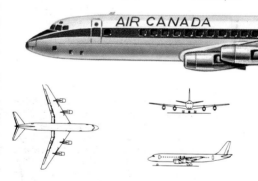

range with max payload 9,950km (6,185mls)

Weights: Basic operating 60,020kg (132,325lb); max weight limited payload 21,092kg (46,500lb); max take-off 147,415kg (325,000lb)

Dimensions: Span 43.41m (142ft 5in); length 45.87m (150ft 6in); height 12.91m (42ft 4in); wing area 266.5m² (2,868sq ft)

Seating Capacity: 117

History: First ordered by Pan American on 13 October 1955, other airlines quickly followed including KLM, SAS and JAL. The original DC-8 Srs 10 was powered by four Pratt & Whitney J57 turbojet engines. First flight was on 30 May 1958, and the DC-8 entered service with both United and Delta on 18 September 1959. The first Srs 50 flew on 20 December 1960, being a Srs 30 airframe but with JT 3D turbofans, which gave greatly improved thrust and fuel economy. A passenger/freight Srs 50 called the Jet Trader first flew on 29 October 1962.

On 28 April 1967 Douglas Aircraft Company merged with the McDonnell Aircraft Company to form McDonnell Douglas Corporation with a work force in excess of 120,000 employees.

143

EMBRAER EMB-110 P-2

Country of Origin: Brazil

Power Plant: Two 559kw (750shp) Pratt & Whitney Aircraft of Canada PT6A-34 turboprops

Performance: Max cruising speed 414km/h (257mph) at 2,440m (8,000ft); economic cruising speed 3 km/h (208mph) at 3,050m (10,000ft); service ceiling 6,860m

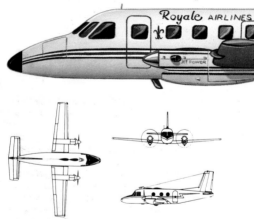

(22,500ft); range with fuel reserves 2,000km (1,243mls)

Weights: Empty equipped 3,555kg (7,837lb); max

take-off 5,670kg (12,500lb)

Dimensions: Span 15.55m (50ft 3.5in); length 15.10m (49ft 6.5in); height 4.92m (16ft 1.75in); wing area 29.10m^2 (313.23sq ft)

Seating Capacity: 21

History: The first production aircraft entered service with the Brazilian Air Force in 1972 with Transbrazil and VASP taking their deliveries in 1973. The EMB-110 Bandeirante was used as a feeder liner to replace Douglas DC-3s and has a seating capacity of 15. First flight of the prototype was on 26 October 1968 and of the production aircraft on 9 August 1972. Notable variants include the 18-passenger EMB-110P, which entered service in 1976. The EMB-110 P-2 had a fuselage stretched by 0.84m (2ft 9in), as did the all-cargo EMB-110K-1 version.

EMBRAER EMB-120 BRASILIA

Country of Origin: Brazil
Production: Number ordered 68; in airline service 26
(42)

Power Plant: Two 1,590shp Pratt & Whitney AC PW115
turboprops

Performance: Max speed 290km/h (108kt); max cruise 584km/h (294kt) at 6,096m (20,000ft); range with max fuel 3,263km (1,760nm)

Weights: Max take-off 10,800kg (23,810lb); max landing 10,550kg (2,325lb); empty 6,835kg (15,068lb)

Dimensions: Span 19.78m (64ft 9in); length 20.00m (65ft 6in); height 6.35m (20ft 8in); wing area 38.03m² (409sq ft)

Seating Capacity: 30

History: The EMB-120 obtained certification in the United States in July 1985 and entered service the following month with Atlantic Southeast. European operation commenced in January 1986 with the West German operator DLT. In addition to the 68 orders there are options for a further 89 to be produced at a rate of 4 per month from 1987.

EMBRAER EMB-121 XINGA

Country of Origin: Brazil
Power Plant: Two Pratt & Whitney (Canada) PT6A-28 turboprops each rated at 680shp for take-off
Performance: Max cruising speed 450km (280mph) at 3,353m (11,000ft); initial rate of climb 7.11m/sec

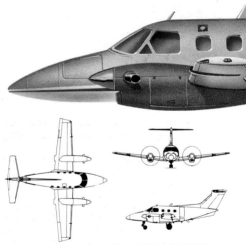

(1,400ft/min); service ceiling 7,925m (26,000ft); max range 2,352km (1,462mls) with payload of 610kg

PP-ZXI B

Weights: Empty operating 3,500kg (7,716lb); max take-off 5,670kg (12,500lb); max landing 5,340kg (11,773lb)

Dimensions: Span 14.45m (47ft 5in); length 12.25m (40ft 2.25in); height 4.74m (15ft 6.5in); wing area 27.50m² (296sq ft)

Seating Capacity: 6

History: The EMB-121 Xinga first flew on 10 October 1976. First deliveries were in 1978, with the first commercial deliveries in June 1979. A derivative of the Embraer Bandeirante, the Xinga is aimed at the executive market. It has a circular pressurized fuselage that is shorter than that of the Bandeirante, a 'T'-tail, more powerful engines and a shorter wing span.

FAIRCHILD FH-227

Country of Origin: Netherlands
Production: Number built 78; in airline service 46
Power Plant: Two 2,300shp Rolls-Royce Dart 532-7L turboprops
Performance: Max cruising speed 473km/h (294mph) at 4,570m (15,000ft); best economy cruise 435km/h

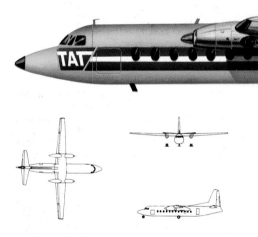

(270mph) at 7620m (25,000ft); initial rate of climb 7.9m/sec (1,560ft/min); service ceiling 8,535m

(28,000ft); range with max payload 1,055km (656mls); range with max fuel 2,660km (1,665mls)

Weights: Empty 10,398kg (22,923lb); max payload 5,080kg (11,200lb); max take-off 19,730kg (43,500lb)

Dimensions: Span 29.0m (95ft 2in); length 25.50m (83ft 8in); height 8.41m (27ft 7in); wing area 70.0m² (754sq ft)

Seating Capacity: 40

History: Fairchild built the FH-227 under a licence agreement with Fokker to meet local demand for the F27 Friendship type. First prototype flew on 27 January 1966 and the first order was placed by Mohawk. The basic FH-227 incorporated a lengthened nose to house weather radar and a stretched fuselage some 1.83m (6ft) longer than the F27.

FOKKER F27 FRIENDSHIP MK 200

Country of Origin: Netherlands
Production: Number ordered 574; in airline service 337 (9)
Power Plant: Two 2,105eshp Rolls-Royce Dart 528 or 528-7E or 2,230eshp Dart 532-7 turboprops
Performance: Cruising speed 486km/h (302mph); initial rate of climb 7.5m/sec (1,475ft/min); service ceil-

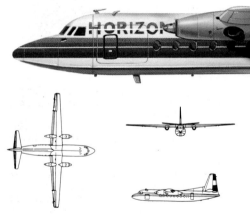

ing 9,000m 29,500ft); range with max payload 2,070km (1,285mls); range with max fuel 2,211km (1,374mls)

Weights: Empty 10,295kg (22,696lb), operating empty 11,159kg (24,600lb); max payload 4,690kg (10,340lb); max take-off 20,410kg (45,000lb)

Dimensions: Span 29.00m (95ft 2in); length 23.56m (77ft 3.5in); height 8.51m (27ft 11in); wing area 70.0sq m (753.5sq ft)

Seating Capacity: 36

History: First flight in prototype form was on 24 November 1955, with a second prototype, 0.91m (3ft) longer, flying on 29 January 1957. First production craft flew on 23 March 1958, these being similar to the second prototype and powered by Dart 511 engines. The F27 Friendship became the best selling turbo-prop transport, outside the Soviet Union, when coupled with the production of the Fairchild FH-227.

FOKKER F28 FELLOWSHIP MK 1000

Country of Origin: Netherlands

Production: Number ordered 237; in airline service 184 (9)

Power Plant: Two 4,468kgp (9,850lb st) Rolls-Royce Spey 555-15 turbofans

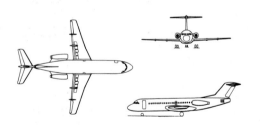

Performance: Max cruising speed 849km/h (528mph) at 6,400m (21,000ft); best economy cruise 836km/h (519mph) at 7,620m (25,000ft); long-range cruise

676km/h (420mph) at 9,150m (30,000ft); max operating ceiling 10,675m (35,000ft); range with max payload 1,538km (956mls); range with max fuel 1,945km (1,208mls)

Weights: Operating empty 16,144kg (35,517lb); max payload 8,936kg (19,700lb); max take-off 29,480kg (65,000lb)

Dimensions: Span 23.58m (77ft 4.25in); length 21.90m (89ft 10.75in); height 8.47m (27ft 9.5in); wing area 76.4sq m (822sq ft)

Seating Capacity: 60

History: The prototype first flew on May 1967 and the first production model on 21 May 1968. The Fellowship entered service with LTU of Germany in February 1969 as a short-haul airliner with five-abreast, one-class seating. This MK 1000 was also offered in a mixed passenger/freight version.

FOKKER F50
Country of Origin: Netherlands

Production: Number ordered 38; in airline service nil (38)

Power Plant: 2 Pratt & Whitney PW124 turboprops, take-off power 2,160shp
Performance: Max cruise 515km/h (278kt) at 6,400m (21,000ft); range with max payload 2,091km (1,129nm); range with max fuel 4,119km (2,224nm)

Weights: Max take-off 20,820kg (45,900lb); max landing 18,990kg (41,865lb); empty 12,633kg (27,850lb)
Dimensions: Span 29m (95ft 1.5in); length 25.25m (82ft 8in); height 8.6m (28ft 6in); wing area 70sq m (754sq ft)
Seating Capacity: 50
History: Launched together with the Fokker 100 programme at the end of 1983, the F50 is Fokker's replacement for the F27 Friendship, which commenced operations in 1958. The F50 retains the same fuselage length, and the first prototype flew on 28 December 1985. Certification is hoped for at the end of 1986 when Fokker are due to commence deliveries to Ansett Transport Industries.

FOKKER F100
Country of Origin: Netherlands

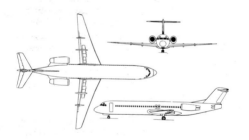

Production: Number ordered 38; in airline service nil (38)
Power Plant: Two 59.3kn (13,320lb) Rolls-Royce Tay 620-15 turbofans

Performance: Max cruise speed 800km/h (432kt) at 10,670m (35,000ft); range with max payload 2,015km (1,099nm); range with max fuel 3,745km (2,022nm)

Weights: Max take-off 41,500kg (91,500lb); max landing 38,330 (84,500lb); operating empty 23,250kg (51,260lb)

Dimensions: Wing span 28.08m (92ft 1.5in); length 35.53m (116ft 6.5in); height 8.5m (27ft 10.5in); wing area 94.30sq m (1,014.7sq ft)

Seating Capacity: 107

History: Launched in late 1983, the sales to date of the Fokker 100 have been encouraging and the aircraft, which has now made its first flight, will be available in mid-1987 and will enter service first with Saxisair. Although production is only set at 3 per month by 1988, this will probably be increased as orders mount. Other airlines who have placed orders include KLM and US Air.

GAF NOMAD N22

Country of Origin: Australia

Power Plant: Two Allison 250-B17B turboprops each rated at 400shp for take-off

Performance: Normal cruising speed 311km/h (193mph); initial rate of climb 7.4m/sec (1,460ft/sec); service ceiling 6,860m (22,500ft); max range 1,352km (840mls)

Weights: Operating weight empty 2,116kg (4,666lb); max take-off 3,855kg (8,500lb)

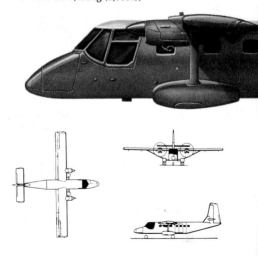

Dimensions: Span 16.46m (54ft 0in); length 12.56m (41ft 2.5in); height 5.52m (18ft 1.5in); wing area 30.10sq m 324sq ft)

Seating capacity: 12

History: First prototype flight was made on 23 July 1971 and the Nomad entered service on 18 December 1975 with Aero Pelican. The fuselage is almost square in cross-section and incorporates large side-loading doors. A stretched fuselage version, 1.14m (3ft 9in) longer, designated N24, entered service in 1976 with additional seating for a further 3 passengers.

GATES LEARJET 24F

Country of Origin: USA

Power Plant: Two General Electric CJ610-6 turbojets each rated at 1,340kgp (2,950lb st) for take-off

Performance: Max operating speed 877km/h

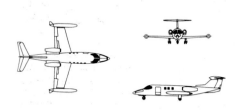

(545mph) at 9,450m (31,000ft); initial rate of climb 34.5m/sec (6,800ft/min); service ceiling 8,230m (27,000ft); range with max payload 2,728km (1,695mls)

Weights: Empty operating 3,234kg (7,130lb); max payload 1,755kg (3,870lb); max take-off weight 6,123kg (13,500lb); max landing weight 5,388kg (11,880lb)

Dimensions: Span 10.84m (35ft 7in); length 13.18m (43ft 3in); height 3.73m (12ft 3in); wing area 21.53sq m (231.8sq ft)

Seating Capacity: 6

History: Designed in Switzerland by William P. Lear as one of the smallest and fastest business jets, the Learjet went into production in 1962. The prototype Learjet 23 first flew on 7 October 1963, and the first deliveries were made in 1964. Just over 100 were manufactured before the model 24 was introduced with uprated engines. The stretched fuselage version, the model 25, first flew on August 1966 with seating capacity for 8 passengers. The 20 series Learjets became the best selling business jets.

GATES LEARJET 55 LONGHORN

Country of Origin: USA
Power Plant: Two Garrett AiResearch TFE 731-3A

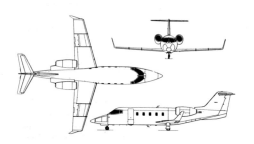

Performance: Max speed 885km/h (550mph); max ceiling 15,550m (51,000ft); initial rate of climb 25.5m/

sec (5,020ft/min); range 7,478km (2,475mls) with 545kg (1,200lb) payload

Weights: Empty operating 4,760kg (12,130lb); max take-off 8,618kg (19,000lb)

Dimensions: Span 13.34m (43ft 9.5in); length 16.79m (55ft 1.5in); height 4.47m (14ft 8in); wing area 24.57m² (264.5sq ft)

Seating Capacity: 10

History: Designed with stand-up headroom, unlike the series 20 and 30 models, the Learjet 55 provides a higher standard of comfort. Put in hand in 1977, it has a cabin length of 4.93m (16ft 2.5in). One drawback of the 55 Longhorn is the 1,708m (5,600ft) of field runway required for take-off compared to the 1,213m (3,977ft) required by the Model 25D.

GRUMMAN GULFSTREAM 1-C
Country of Origin: USA
Production: Number built 200

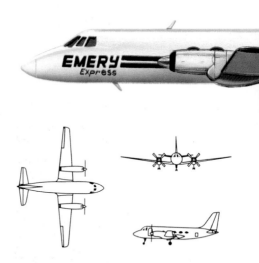

Power Plant: Two Rolls-Royce Dart RD27 Mk 529-8X
Performance: Max cruising speed 560km/h (348mph); initial rate of climb 9.6m/sec (1,900ft/min); service

ceiling 10,240m (33,600ft); range with max fuel 4,058km (2,540mls)

Weights: Empty operating 11,295kg (24,850lb); max take-off 16,363kg (36,000lb); max landing 15,584kg (34,285lb)

Dimensions: Span 23.92m (78ft 6in); length 22.96m (75ft 4in); height 7.01m (23ft); wing area 56.7m² (610.3sq ft)

Seating Capacity: 37

History: Originating in 1956 as a large executive aircraft, the first flight was on 14 August 1958, and deliveries commenced in 1959. Production of the 10-seat model ended in February 1969 when it gave way to the Gulfstream II. In 1979 Gulfstream American started production on a 32-38-seat commuter version, and conversions are now available with a fuselage lengthened by 3.25m (10ft 8in).

GRUMMAN GULFSTREAM II

Country of Origin: USA
Power Plant: Two Rolls-Royce Spey Mk 511-8 turbofans each rated at 5,175kgp (11,400lb st) for take-off
Performance: Max cruising speed 936km/h (581mph)

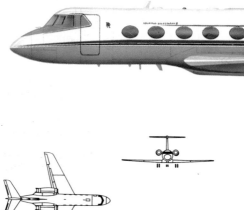

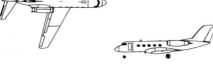

at 7,620m (25,000ft); initial rate of climb 22.1m/sec (4,350ft/min); service ceiling 13,100m (43,000ft); range with max fuel 6,880km (4,275mls)

Weights: Empty operating 16,737kg (36,900lb); max take-off 29,711kg (65,500lb); max loading 26,535kg (58,500lb)

Dimensions: Span 20.98m (68ft 10in); length 24.36m (79ft 11in); height 7.47m (24ft 6in); wing area 75.21m² (809.6sq ft)

Seating Capacity: 10

History: Launched in May 1965 to succeed the Gulfstream I, the Gulfstream II was of similar dimensions but with seating capacity of up to 19 in high-density layout. Flight tested on 2 October 1966, and aimed at the top end of the market, it entered service in December 1966. In 1978 optional tip tanks were made available adding almost 1,000km (621mls) to the range.

HANDLEY PAGE HERALD 200

Country of Origin: United Kingdom
Production: Number built 50; in airline service 16
Power Plant: Two 2,105ehp Rolls-Royce Dart 527 turboprops

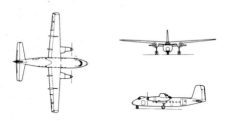

Performance: Max cruising speed 441km/h (274mph) at 4,572m (15,000ft); best economy cruise 426km/h (265mph) at 7,010m (23,000ft); initial rate of climb 9.1m/sec (1,805ft/min); service ceiling 8,504m

(27,900ft); range with max payload 1,786km (1,110mls); range with max fuel 2,607km (1,620mls)

Weights: Operating empty 11,700kg (25,800lb); max payload 5,100kg (11,242lb); max take-off 19,505kg (43,000lb)

Dimensions: Span 28.88m (94ft 9in); length 23.01m (75ft 6in); height 7.34m (24ft 1in); wing area 82.3m² (886sq ft)

Seating Capacity: 44

History: Originally designed as a piston-engined feeder-line aircraft to seat 44 passengers, the Herald finally entered production with Dart turboprops. The two prototypes first flew on 25 August 1955. The Srs 200 was 1.09m (3ft 7in) longer and accommodated an additional 4 passengers. The first production Srs 200 flew on 13 December 1961, and entered service with Jersey Airlines the following month. Handley Page ceased operating in 1970.

ILYUSHIN IL-14M

Country of Origin: Soviet Union
Production: Number built 3,500; in airline service 265 plus

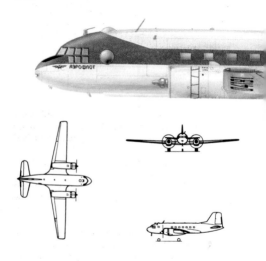

Power Plant: Two 1,900hp Shvetsov ASh-82T 14-cylinder radial air-cooled engines
Performance: Max speed 417km/h (259mph); high-speed cruise 385km/h (239mph); long-range cruise

311km/h (193mph); initial climb rate 6.2m/sec (1,220ft/min); service ceiling 6,705m (22,000ft); range with max payload 1,034km (810mls), with max fuel 3,202km (1,988mls)

Weights: Operational equipped 12,600kg (27,776lb); max take-off 18,000kg (39,683mls)

Dimensions: Span 31.69m (104ft 0in); length 22.30m (73ft 2in); height 7.90m (25ft 11in); wing area 99.70m² (1,075sq ft)

Seating Capacity: 24-28

History: First flown as a prototype in 1952, this was the first post-WWII Ilyushm to enter production. The Il-14P was the initial variant and entered service both with Aeroflot as a 26-passenger airliner, and with the Military. The Il-14M first flew in 1956 with a stretched fuselage of 1.0m (3ft 4in) able to accommodate an additional 2 passengers.

ILYUSHIN IL-18D

Country of Origin: Soviet Union

Production: Number built 656; in airline service 177 plus

Power Plant: Four Ivchenko A1-20 M turboprops each rated at 4,250ehp

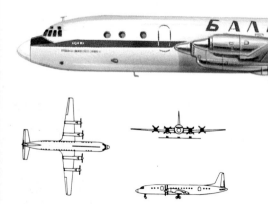

Performance: Max cruise (at max take-off weight) 675km/h (419mph); economy cruise 625km/h (388mph); operating altitude 8,000-10,000m (26,250-32,800ft); range (max payload and one hour's reserves) 3,700km (2,300mls), (max fuel and one

hour's reserves) 6,500km (4,040mls)

Weights: Empty equipped (90-seater) 35,000kg (77,160lb); max take-off 64,000kg (141,000lb)

Dimensions: Span 37.40m (122ft 8.5in); length 35.90m (117ft 9in); height 10.17m (33ft 4in); wing area 140m² (1,507sq ft)

Seating Capacity: 110

History: The prototype Il-18 first flew in July 1955, and the airliner entered service with Aeroflot on 20 April 1959. It was originally produced as the Il-18A with either Kuznetsov NK-4 or Ivchenko Al-20K engines and seating capacity of 75, but when the Il-18B was introduced with an increased seating capacity of 84, the Ivchenko engines became standard. In 1961 the 89/100-passenger variant Il-18V was introduced, and in 1965 the Il-18I entered service.

ILYUSHIN IL-62 CLASSIC

Country of Origin: Soviet Union
Production: Number built 226 plus; in airline service 209 plus
Power Plant: Four 10,500kgp (23,150lb st) Kuznetsov NK-8-4 turbofans

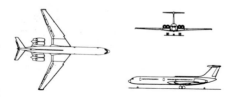

Performance: Typical cruising speed 850-900km/h (528-560mph) at 10,000-12,000m (33,000-39,400ft); initial climb rate 18m/sec (3,540ft/min); take-off distance required 3,250m (10,660ft); landing distance required 2,800m (9,185ft); range with max payload, and 1-hr fuel reserve 6,700km (4,160mls); range with max fuel 9,200km (5,715mls)

Weights: Operating weight empty 69,400kg (153,000lb); max payload 23,000kg (50,700lb); max fuel load 83,325kg (183,700lb); max take-off 162,000kg 9357,000lb); max landing 105,000kg (232,000lb); max zero-fuel weight 93,500kg (206,000lb)

Dimensions: Span 43.20m (141ft 9in); length 53.12m (174ft 3.5in); height 12.35m (40ft 6.25in); wing area 279.6m² (3,010sq ft)

Seating Capacity: 168

History: The Il-62 was the first long-range four-engined jet developed by the Soviet Union for commercial use. The contemporary of the Boeing 707, the DC-10 and the VC10, it entered service with Aeroflot on 15 September 1967 and still remains in very limited production. First used on the Moscow-Montreal route, the Il-62 replaced the Tu-114s on the Moscow-New York route in 1968.

ILYUSHIN IL-76 T 'CANDID'

Country of Origin: Soviet Union
Production: Number built 400 plus; in airline service 141 plus
Power Plant: Four Soloviev D-30KP turbofans each rated at 12,000kgp (26,455lb st) for take-off
Performance: Typical cruising speed 850km/h (528mph) at 13,000m (42,650ft); take-off run, unpaved

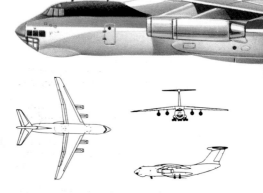

runway 850m (2,790ft); landing run, unpaved runway 450m (1,476ft); typical range with max payload 5,000km (3,100mls)
Weights: Max payload 40,000kg (88,185lb); max take-

off weight 157,000kg (346,125lb)

Dimensions: Span 50.50m (165ft 8in); length 46.59m (152ft 10.5in); height 14.76m 948ft 5in); wing area 300.0m² (3,229.2sq ft)

History: First flown in March 1971, the Il-76 Candid, although performing 'national economy' duties with the Aeroflot operation (Il-76T variant), is primarily a specialized freighter used by the Soviet Air Force (Il-76M variant). It is expected to perform tanker duties for flight refuelling and also to be the basis for an airborne warning and control system, and although flight-tested for both these roles it is not yet thought to be in squadron service. Some 20 variants are thought to have been produced and the aircraft is currently in service with 4 Middle East airlines in addition to Aeroflot and Cubana.

ILYUSHIN IL-86 'CAMBER'

Country of Origin: Soviet Union
Production: Number built 80 plus; in airline service 80 plus

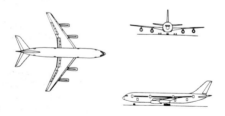

Power Plant: Four Kuznetsov NK-86 turbofans each rated at 13,000kgp (28,635lb st) for take-off
Performance: Cruising speed 900-950km/h (560-

590mph) at 9,000m (30,000ft); range 3,600km (2,235mls) with full passenger payload

Weights: Max payload 42,000kg (92,500lb); gross weight 206,000kg (454,145lb)

Dimensions: Span 48.06m (157ft 8.25in); length 5,954m (195ft 4in); height 15.81m (51ft 10.5in); wing area 320m² (3,444sq ft)

Seating Capacity: 350

History: The first and only Soviet wide-body commercial aircraft, the Il-86 first flew in December 1976 and entered service with Aeroflot in December 1980. The An-124 wide-bodied freighter is currently undergoing flight tests and may be expected to enter service before 1990 using Lotarev D-18T engines with 51,650lb thrust which are also expected to power the long range Il-96 in the 1990s.

IAI WESTWIND 1124

Country of Origin: Israel

Production: Number produced 53

Power Plant: Two Garrett AiResearch TFE 731-3 turbofans each rated at 1,680kgp (3,700lb st) for take-off

Performance: Max speed 872km/h (542mph); service ceiling 13,725m (45,000ft); max range 4,448km (2,765mls)

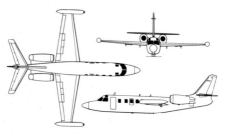

Weights: Empty operating 5,806kg (12,800lb); max take-off 10,364kg (22,850lb); max landing 8,618kg (19,000lb)

Dimensions; Span 13.65m (44ft 9.5in); length 15.93m

(52ft 3in); height 4.81m (15ft 9.5in); wing area 28.64m² (308.3sq ft)

Seating Capacity: 10

History: First flown in the USA as the Aero Commander Model 1121 on 27 January 1963 powered by General Electric CJ610-1 turbojets. The first production craft flew on 5 October 1964 and entered service in January 1965 as a 7-seat business jet. North America bought out the Aero Commander company and sold off the Model 1121 to Israel Aircraft Industries in 1967 because of conflict with North America's own Jet Commander and Sabreliner aircraft. IAI stretched the fuselage, and the 1123 first flew on 28 September 1970 powered by CJ610-9 turbojets. Production of the 1123 ended in 1976, being replaced with the 1124 Westwind which had first flown on 21 July 1975.

LET L-410A TURBOLET

Country of Origin: Czechoslovakia
Production: Number produced 650 plus
Power Plant: Two 715eshp Pratt & Whitney (VACL) PT6A-27 turboprops
Performance: Max cruising speed 370km/h (230mph) at 3,000m (9840ft); best economy cruise 360km/h

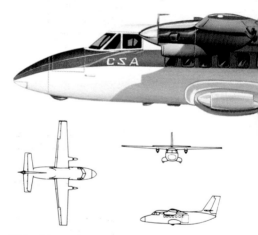

(224mph); initial rate of climb 8.2m/sec (1,610ft/min); service ceiling 7,100m (23,300ft); range with max payload 300km (186mls); range with max fuel 1300km

OK-ADO

(807mls)

Weights: Operating empty 3,100kg (6,834lb); max take-off 5,700kg (12,566lb); max landing 5,500kg (12,125lb)

Dimensions: Span 17.48m (57ft 4.5in); length 13.61m (44ft 7.75in); height 5.65m (18ft 6.5in); wing area 32.86m² (353.7sq ft)

Seating Capacity: 15

History: Developed by the Czechoslovakian National Aircraft Industry, the L-410 was to have been powered by Czech-built M-601 engines, but these were not ready in time and the prototype flew with Pratt & Whitney PT6A-27s on 16 April 1975.

LOCKHEED ELECTRA L-188A

Country of Origin: USA
Production: Number built 187; in airline service 84
Power Plant: Four 3,750ehp Allison 501-D13A turboprops
Performance: Max cruising speed 652km/h (405mph) at 6,700m (22,000ft); best economy cruise 602km/h

(374mph); initial rate of climb 8.5m/sec (1,670ft/min); service ceiling 8,230m (27,000ft); range with max payload 3,540km (2,200mls); range with max fuel 4,023km (2,500mls)

Weights: Basic operating 27,895kg (61,500lb); max payload 10,350kg (22,825lb); max take-off 52,664kg (116,000lb)

Dimensions: Span 30.18m (99ft 0in); length 31.81m (104ft 6in); height 10.0m (32ft 10in); wing area 120.8m² (1,300sq ft)

Seating Capacity: 100

History: Initiated as a short/medium-range transport for the US domestic market by America Airlines in 1954, both America and Eastern Airlines placed orders in mid-1955. First flight was on 6 December 1967, and the Electra entered service with Eastern on 12 January 1959 and with America 11 days later, by which time almost 150 had been ordered. The Electra was to be the only US-designed and produced turboprop to operate regular services.

LOCKHEED L-100-30 HERCULES

Country of Origin: USA

Production: Number built (civil version) 102; in airline service 57

Power Plant: Four 4,508eshp Allison 501-D22A turboprops

Performance: Max cruising speed 607km/h (377mph); initial rate of climb 9.65m/sec (1,900ft/min); range with max payload 3,425km (2,130mls); range with max

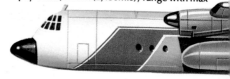

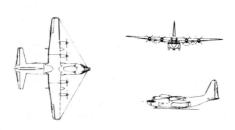

PK-PLR

fuel 7,630km (4,740mls)

Weights: Operating empty 32,386kg (71,400lb); max payload 23,315kg (51,400lb); max take-off 70,308kg (155,000lb)

Dimensions: Span 40.41m (132ft 7in); length 34.35m (112ft 8.5in); height 11.66m (38ft 3in); wing area 162.12m² (1,745sq ft)

History: The civilian version, the L-100-20, was a stretched-fuselage variant (2.54m (100in) longer) of the basic military C-130. First flight was on 19 April 1968, with certification following later that year. In 1969 orders were placed by Saturn Airways for a version with a fuselage stretched 2.03m (80in) farther; this first flew on 14 August 1970 and was designated L-100-30.

LOCKHEED JETSTAR II

Country of Origin: USA
Power Plant: Four Garrett AiResearch TFE731-3 turbofans each rated at 1,680kgp (3,700lb st) for take-off
Performance: Max cruising speed 880km/h (547mph) at 9,145m (30,000ft); initial rate of climb 21.3m/sec (4,200ft/min); service ceiling 11,580m (38,000ft);

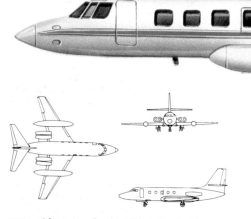

range with max payload 4,818km (2,994mls)
Weights: Empty operating 10,967kg (24,178lb); max payload 1,280kg (2,822lb); max take-off 19,844kg

(43,750lb); max landing 16,329kg (36,000lb)

Dimensions: Span 16.60m (54ft 5in); length 18.42m (60ft 5in); height 6.23m (20ft 5in); wing area 50.40m² (542.5sq ft)

Seating Capacity: 10

History: Production of the Jetstar I lasted for 13 years, terminating in 1973 after 162 had been produced. AiResearch developed a conversion kit in 1973 using TFE 731-1 turbofans. A prototype flew on 10 July 1974 and the first production conversion, designated Jetstar 731, flew on 18 March 1976. Lockheed subsequently recommenced manufacture using the TFE 731-3 engines. The prototype of the Jetstar II first flew on 18 August 1976 and deliveries commenced the following year.

LOCKHEED L-1011-1 TRISTAR

Country of Origin: USA
Production: Number built 250; in airline service 230
Power Plant: Three 19,050kgp (42,000lb st) Rolls-Royce RB211-22B or 19,730kgp (43,500lb st) RB211-22F turbofans
Performance: Max cruising speed 925km/h (575mph) — Mach 0.85 at 10,670m (35,000ft); best range cruise

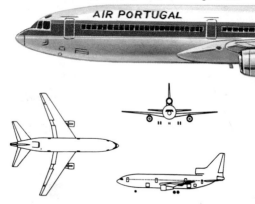

875km/h (544mph) — Mach 0.82 at 10,670m (35,000ft); initial rate of climb 14.3m/sec (2,800ft/min); service ceiling 12.800m (42,000ft); range with max payload 4,629km (2,878mls); range with max fuel 7,189km

(4,467mls), with payload of 18,145kg (40,000lb)

Weights: Operating empty 106,265kg (234,275lb); max payload 41,150kg (90,725lb); max take-off 195,045kg (430,000lb)

Dimensions: Span 47.34m (155ft 4in); length 54.35m (178ft 8in); height 16.87m (55ft 4in); wing area 320.0m² (3,456sq ft)

Seating Capacity: 345

History: The first prototype Tristar flew on 17 November 1970, and deliveries commenced to Eastern on 5 April 1972. Eastern inaugurated services with them on 26 April, two months ahead of TWA. The final two Tristars were delivered in June 1985, bringing to an end a project that saw Lockheed on the brink of bankruptcy (they had lost $10 million on every aircraft delivered) and led Rolls-Royce into bankruptcy.

McDONNELL DOUGLAS DC-8 SUPER 70 Srs
Country of Origin: USA

Production: Number available 234; in airline service 104

Power Plant: Four 10,886kg (24,000lb) thrust General Electric/SNECMA CFM56-2 turbofans

Performance: Max speed 966km/h (600mph); cruising speed 855km/h (531mph) at 10,670m (35,000ft); range with max payload 11,619km (7,220mls)

Weights: Empty operating 69,218kg (152,600lb); max take-off 151,953kg (335,000lb)

Dimensions: Span 45.24m (148ft 5in); length 47.98m (157ft 5in); height 12.93m (42ft 5in); wing area 271.92m² (2,927.0sq ft)

Seating Capacity: 189

History: In 1979 Commacorp in association with McDonnell Douglas launched a refit programme on Srs 60 DC-8s. The refit cost of $17.5 million included a lighter, more efficient, Garrett-AiResearch dual-air-cycle system, in addition to the GE/SNECMA CFM56-2 engines, which are some 23 per cent more efficient. The first modernized, re-engined DC-8 flew in August 1981.

McDONNELL DOUGLAS DC-9 Srs 50

Country of Origin: USA
Production: Number ordered, all DC-9s, 1,390; in airline service 1,126 (100)

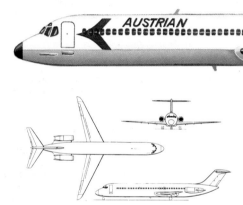

Power Plant: Two 7,031kg (15,500lb) thrust Pratt & Whitney JT8D-15 turbofans
Performance: Max speed 925km/h (575mph); economic cruising speed 821km/h (510mph); range with passengers and fuel reserves 3,323km (2,065mls)
Weights: Empty 28,068kg (61,880lb); max take-off 54,885kg (121,000lb)

Dimensions: Span 28.47m (93ft 5in); length 40.72m (133ft 7.25in); height 8.53m (28ft 0in); wing area 92.97m² (1,000.75sq ft)

Seating Capacity: 139

History: Douglas first announced their decision to proceed with a newly designed 90-seater aircraft on 8 April 1963. Unlike the DC-8, the DC-9 was aimed primarily at the short-haul market and was to have tail-mounted engines like the BAC One-Eleven. First flight was on 25 February 1965, and the DC-9 Srs 10 powered by Pratt & Whitney JT8D-5 engines entered service with Delta on 8 December 1965. The Srs 30, with a fuselage stretched by 4.6m (14ft 11in) and with extended wing tips, first flew on 1 August 1967. The Srs 40 was developed specifically for SAS, and which was 1.87m (6ft 4in) longer still; it first flew on 28 November 1967. The Srs 50, which was 1.87m (6ft 4in) longer than the Srs 40, made its first flight on 17 December 1974 and entered service with Swissair on 24 August 1975.

McDONNELL DOUGLAS DC-9 SUPER 80 (MD-80)

Country of Origin: USA

Production: Number ordered (all MD-80 series) 506; in airline service 317 (157). 189 (Number ordered excludes Chinese co-production of 25 DC-9-80)

Power Plant: Two 8,400kgp (18,500lb st) Pratt & Whitney JT8D-209 turbofans

Performance: Max cruising speed 878km/h (546mph)

at 9,450m (31,000ft); range with 137 passenger load 3,306km (2,055st mls) at 10,668m (35,000ft)

Weights: Operating weight empty 35,270kg (77,757lb); max take-off weight 63,503kg (140,000lb); max landing weight 58,060kg (128,000lb); max zero fuel weight 53,524kg (118,000lb)

Dimensions: Span 32.85m (107ft 10in); length 45.08m (147ft 10in); height 8.93m (29ft 10in); wing area 118.8m² (1,279sq ft)

Seating Capacity: 150

History: McDonnell Douglas continued development of the DC-9, and between 1975 and 1977 experimented with JT8D-209 engines and increased fuselage lengths. The eventual outcome was designated DC-9 Srs 55 in 1977, but entered production redesignated DC-9 Super 80, the first flight of which was in October 1979. The DC-9 entered service in 1980 with Swissair and was renamed yet again, this time as the MD-80.

McDONNELL DOUGLAS DC-10 Srs 30

Country of Origin: USA
Production: Number ordered 437; in airline service 401 (8)
Power Plant: Three 23,134kgp (51,000lb st) General Electric CF6-50C turbofans
Performance: Max cruising speed at 9,450m (31,000ft),

917km/h (570mph); initial rate of climb 11.8m/sec (2,320ft/min); service ceiling 9,965m (32,700ft); range with max payload 6,875km (4,272mls); range with max fuel 11,118km (6,910mls)

Weights: Basic operating 119,334kg (263,087lb); max payload 47,587kg (104,913lb); max take-off 251,744kg (555,000lb)

Dimensions: Span 40.42m (165ft 4in); length 55.35m (181ft 7in); height 17.7m (58ft 1in); wing area 364.3m² (3,921sq ft)

Seating capacity: 380

History: A transcontinental trijet developed to compete with Boeing's 747, the first orders were placed by American on 19 February 1968 and by United two months later. First flight was on 29 August 1970, and the DC-10 entered service with American Airlines on 5 August 1971 between Los Angeles and Chicago. The DC-10 Srs 30 was developed for European Airlines and has a wing span increased by 3.08m (10ft) and a fractionally shorter fuselage.

McDONNELL DOUGLAS MD-83

Country of Origin: United States
Power Plant: Two 96.5kN (21,700lb) Pratt & Whitney
JT8D-219 turbofan

Performance: Max speed 283km/h (153kt); max cruise
924km/h (499kt) at 8,230m (27,000ft); range with max
payload 3,445km (1,860nm); range with max fuel
4,941km (2,668nm)

Weights: Max take-off 72,580kg (160,000lb); max landing 63,280kg (139,500lb); empty operating 36,620kg (80,230lb)

Dimensions: Span 32.9m (107ft 10in); length 45m (147ft 11in); height 9m (29ft 7in); wing area 112.3m² (1,209sq ft)

Seating capacity: 172

History: The longer-range version and heaviest of the McDonnell Douglas MD-80 family of airliners, the MD-83 entered service in February 1986. Using the latest new technology, McDonnell Douglas created a best selling range out of an existing design. The DC-9, MD-81, MD-82 and MD-83 are all dimensionally the same but with engine and weight differences. The MD-87, which received its go-ahead in January 1986 for 1987 delivery, is 5.25m (7ft 6in) shorter, seating 139 passengers. It had its maiden flight on 4 December 1986.

MARTIN 404

Country of Origin: USA
Production: Number built 103; in airline service 15

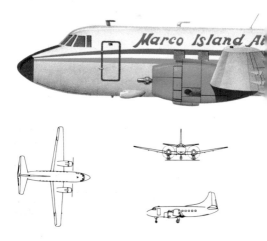

Power Plant: Two 2,400 hp Pratt & Whitney R-2800-CB-16 Double Wasp piston engines
Performance: Max speed 500km/h (312mph) at 4,420m (14,500ft); typical cruise 442km/h (276mph) at 5,486m (18,000ft); initial rate of climb 9.6m/sec (1,905ft/min);

service ceiling 8,845m (29,000ft); range with payload of 4,633kg (10,205lb), 500km (310mls); range with max fuel 1,715km (1,070mls)

Weights: Empty equipped 13,223kg (29,126lb); max payload 5,263kg (11,692lb); max take-off 20,385kg (44,900lb); max landing 19,522kg (43,000lb)

Dimensions: Span 28.44m (93ft 3.5in); length 22.75m (74ft 7in); height 8.61m (28ft 2in); wing area 79.89m² (864sq ft)

Seating Capacity: 48-52

History: Launched initially as the Martin 202. Designed as a short-range transport to replace the DC-3, only 43 aircraft were built. An improved variant, the 404, first flew on 21 October 1950 and entered service with TWA on 5 October 1951.

MITSUBISHI MU-2

Country of Origin: Japan

Power Plant: Two Garrett AiResearch TPE331-6-251M turboprops each rated at 724ehp for take-off

Performance: Max cruising speed 589km/h (365mph); initial rate of climb 14.5m/sec (2,840ft/min); service

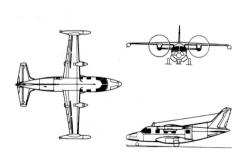

ceiling 9,815m (32,200ft); max range 2,705km
(1,680mls)

Weights: Empty operating 3,113kg (6,864lb); max
take-off 4,750kg (10,470lb); max landing 4,515kg
(9,955lb)

Dimensions: Span 11.94m (39ft 2in); length 10.13m
(33ft 3in); height 3.94m (12ft 11in); wing area 16.55m²
(178sq ft)

Seating Capacity: 7

History: First prototype flew on 14 September 1963,
powered by Turbomeca Astazon engines. The first
production craft, powered by the TPE 331-6 engines,
on 11 March 1965. The MU-2G, a stretched-fuselage
version, capable of carrying an additional 2 passengers, first flew on 10 January 1969.

NAMC YS-11A

Country of Origin: Japan
Production: Number built 182; in airline service 118
Power Plant: Two 3,060hp Rolls-Royce Dart 542-10K turboprops
Performance: Max cruising speed at 4,575m (15,000ft),

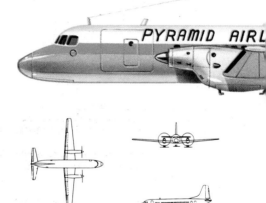

469km/h (291mph); best economy cruise at 6,100m (20,000ft), 452km/h (281mph); initial rate of climb 6.2m/sec (1,220ft/min); service ceiling 6,980m (22,900ft); range with max payload 1,090km (680mls);

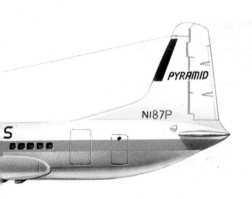

range with max fuel 3,215km(2,000mls)

Weights: Operating empty 15,419kg (33,993lb); max payload 6,581kg (14,508lb); max take-off 24,500kg (54,010lb)

Dimensions: Span 32.00m (104ft 11.75in); length 26.30m (86ft 3.5in); height 8.98m (29ft 5.5in); wing area 94.8m² (1,020.4sq ft)

Seating Capacity: 60

History: The first Japanese-designed and produced commercial aircraft to enter production, the NAMC YS-11 short-to-medium airliner was launched in 1956, with the first prototype flying on 30 August 1962. First production aircraft flew on 23 October 1964 and entered service with Toa Airlines in April 1965. The YS-11A, was produced specifically for North America.

PIPER PA-31T CHEYENNE II
Country of Origin: USA
Power Plant: Two Pratt & Whitney (Canada) PT6A-28 turboprops, each rated at 620eshp for take-off

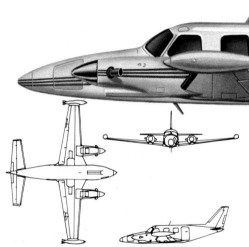

Performance: Max cruising speed 525km/h (326mph) at 3,355m (11,000ft); initial rate of climb 14.2m/sec (2,800ft/min); service ceiling 8,840m (29,000ft); max range 2,08-2,739km (1.621-1,702mls)

Weights: Empty operating 2,209kg (4,870lb); max take-off and landing 4,082kg (9,000lb)

Dimensions: Span 13.01m (42ft 8.25in); length 10.57m (34ft 8in); height 3.89m (12ft 9in); wing area 21.3m² (229sq ft)

Seating Capacity: 6

History: A turboprop version of the Navajo, the Cheyenne first flew on 20 August 1969 and entered service in 1974. It was Piper's first turbine-engined business aircraft. The first production aircraft, designated Cheyenne II, flew on 22 October 1973. The Cheyenne I was introduced in 1977 as a low-cost variant powered by Pratt & Whitney PT6A-11 engines.

PIPER PA-34 SENECA

Country of Origin: USA

Power Plant: Two oppositely-rotating Continental TS10-360-E flat four piston engines each rated at 200hp for take-off

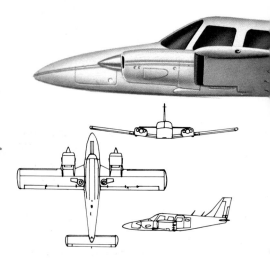

Performance: Max speed 367km/h (228mph) at 4,265m (14,000ft); initial rate of climb 6.8m/sec (1,340ft/min); service ceiling 7,620m (25,000ft); max range 1,007-

1128km (626-701mls)

Weights: Empty operating 1,264kg (2,788lb); max take-off 2,073kg (4,570lb); max landing 1,969kg (4,342lb)

Dimensions: Span 11.85m (38ft 10.75in); length 8.73m (28ft 7.5in); height 3.02m (9ft 10.75in); wing area 19.39sq m (208.7sq ft)

Seating Capacity: 6

History: First flew in 1970, with deliveries commencing the following year. The Seneca is virtually a twin-engined version of the PA-32 Cherokee 6 with a baggage compartment incorporated in a new nose cone. A refined version, the Seneca II, appeared in 1975 as well as a freight variant with a loading door in the fuselage side.

ROCKWELL SABRELINER 75A

Country of Origin: USA

Power Plant: Two General Electric CF700-2D-2 turbofans each rated at 2,043kgp (4,500lb st) for take-off

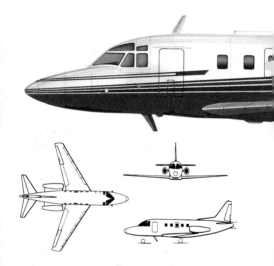

Performance: Max cruising speed 906km/h (563mph); initial rate of climb 22.9m/sec (4,500ft/min); max range 3,156km (1,960)

Weights: Operating empty 5,896kg (13,000lb); max take-off 10,580kg (23,300lb); max landing 9,988kg (22,000lb)

Dimensions: Span 13.62m (44ft 8in); length 14.34m (47ft 0in); height 5.26m (17ft 3in); wing area 31.78sq m (342.05sq ft)

Seating Capacity: 9

History: Originally built to meet USAF requirements for a small trainer/transport, 200 craft were initially built for the USAF and USN. The stretched-fuselage Sabreliner 60 powered by JT12A-8 engines appeared in 1967, and the Sabreliner 70 in 1970, both designed to accommodate 2 additional passengers. The Sabreliner 70 was redesignated 75 and in 1973 the 75A, powered by the GE CF700-2D-2 turbofans.

SAAB SF 340

Country of Origin: Sweden

Production: Number ordered 85; in airline service 33 (41)

Power Plant: Two 1,735shp GE CT7-5A1 turboprops

Performance: Max speed 206km/h (111kt); max cruise

500km/h (270kt) at 4,572m (15,000ft); range with max payload 1,191km (643 m); range with max fuel 3,332km (1,798 m)

Weights: Max take-off 12,372kg (27,275lb); max landing 12,020kg (26,500lb); empty operating 7,899kg (17,415lb)

Dimensions: Span 21.44m (70ft 4in); length 19.42m (67ft 9in); height 6.87m (22ft 6in); wing area 41.81sq m (450sq ft)

Seating Capacity: 35

History: Intended specifically for the short-haul commuter market, the 340 was designed to be easily maintained and operated. A joint development between Saab and Fairchild, announced in 1980, the first 340 flew in January 1983. In 1985 Fairchild withdrew and Saab took over all financial obligations, retaining Fairchild as a subcontractor until early 1987 after the completion of aircraft number 109.

SHORTS SKYVAN

Country of Origin: United Kingdom
Power Plant: Two Garrett-AiResearch TPE331-201 turboprops each rated at 715shp for take-off

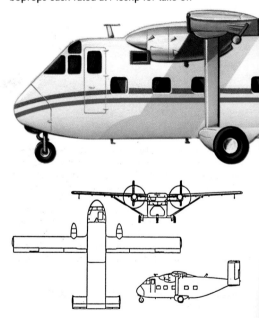

G-BIOH

Performance: Max cruising speed 327km/h (203mph); initial rate of climb 8.3m/sec (1,640ft/min); service ceiling 6,858m (22,500ft); range up to 1,115km (694mls); range with 1,814kg (4,000lb) of freight 300km (187mls)

Weights: Basic operating 3,331kg (7,344lb); max payload 2,086kg (4,600lb); max take-off weight 5,670kg (12,500lb)

Dimensions: Span 19.79m (64ft 11in); length 12.21m (40ft 1in); height 4.60m (15ft 1in); wing area 34.65sq m (373sq ft)

Seating Capacity: 19

History: A small utility transport that first flew on 2 October 1963.

SHORTS 330

Country of Origin: United Kingdom
Production: Number ordered 172; in airline service 120

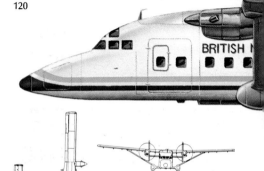

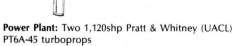

Power Plant: Two 1,120shp Pratt & Whitney (UACL) PT6A-45 turboprops
Performance: Max cruising speed 367km/h (228mph) at 3,280m (10,000ft); long-range cruise 296km/h (184mph); initial rate of climb 6.5m/sec (1,280ft/min);

range with max payload 805km (500mls) with 30 passengers at long-range cruise speed, with 20 passengers at long-range cruise speed 1,400km (870mls)

Weights: Empty equipped 5,753kg (12,685lb); design max payload 3,400kg (7,500lb); max take-off 9,979kg (22,000lb)

Dimensions: Span 22.78m (74ft 9in); length 17.69m (58ft 0.5in); height 4.78m (15ft 8in); wing area 42.1sq m (453sq ft)

Seating Capacity: 30

History: First flown on 22 August 1974, the 330 is derived from the Skyvan STOL utility transport which had itself flown in 1963. First orders were placed by Command Airways of USA and Time Air of Canada, and the 330 entered service with Time Air on 24 August 1976. A rear-loading variant designated UTT is used by the USAF in Europe, which is expected to place further large orders for the type.

SHORTS 360 ADVANCED

Country of Origin: United Kingdom

Production: Number ordered 120 plus; in airline service 90

Power Plant: Two 1,424shp PWAC PT6A-65AR turboprops

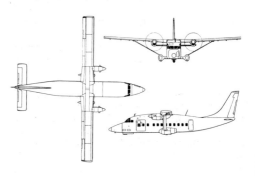

Performance: Max speed 195km/h (105kt); max cruise 393km/h (212kt) at 3,048m (10,000ft); range with max payload 417km (225nm); range with max fuel 1,596km (861nm)

Weights: Max take-off 11,999kg (26,453lb); max landing 11,839kg (26,100lb)

Dimension: Span 22.78m (74ft 9in); length 21.58m (70ft 8in); height 7.21m (23ft 7in); wing area 40.1sq m (453sq ft)

Seating Capacity: 36

History: A larger stable-mate of the Belfast-built Shorts 330, the 360 is now the better seller. Retaining the same high wing and nose, the fuselage is some 75 per cent longer and the twin tail of the 330 is replaced by a conventional single tail. The aircraft first entered service with Thai Airways.

TUPOLEV TU-104A

Country of Origin: Soviet Union
Production: Number produced 200 plus
Power Plant: Two 9,700kgp (21,385lb st) Mikulin AM-3M 500 turbojets

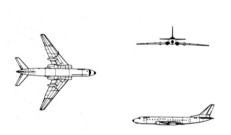

Performance: Max cruising speed 900km/h (560mph); best economy cruise 800km/h (497mph); service ceil-

ing 11,500m (37,750ft); range with max payload at 10,000m (33,000ft), 2,650km (1,645mls); range with max fuel 3,100km (1,925mls)

Weights: Empty 41,600kg (91,710lb); max payload 900kg (19,840lb); max take-off 76,000kg (167,550lb)

Dimensions: Span 34.54m (113ft 4in); length 25.85m (127ft 5in); height 11.90 (39ft 0in); wing area 174.4sq m (1,877sq ft)

Seating Capacity: 70

History: The TU-104 entered service in 1956, the second jet airliner in the world after the Comet, marking the emergence of Aeroflot as a modern international airline. Based on the TU-16 bomber, it had the same wings and tail units, and accommodated 50 passengers. The TU-104A with uprated engines entered service in 1958, followed by the TU-104V with a slightly stretched fuselage and with 100 seats.

TUPOLEV TU-124

Country of Origin: Soviet Union
Production: Number produced 180
Power Plant: Two 5,400kg (11,905lb) Soloviev D-20P turbofans.

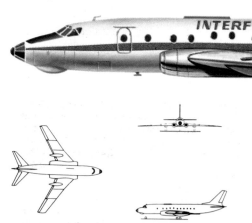

Performance: Max speed 907km/h (603mph); max cruising speed 870km/h (540mph); economical cruise speed 800km/h (497mph) at 10,000m (33,000ft); range with max payload 1,220km (760mls); range with max

fuel and 3,500kg (7,715lb) payload 2,100km (1,305mls)
Weights: Empty 22,500kg (49,600lb); max payload
6,000kg (13,228lb); max take-off weight 38,000kg
(83,775lb); max landing weight 35,000kg (77,160lb)
Dimensions: Span 25.55m (83ft 9.5in); length 30.58m
(100ft 4in); height 8.08m (26ft 6in); wing area 119sq m
(1,281sq ft)
Seating Capacity: 44
History: First flown in June 1960, the TU-124 entered
service with Aeroflot on 2 October 1962 on the
Moscow-Tallinn route. The TU-124 was the first airliner in service powered by turbofan engines. A completely restructured design, the TU-124 looked
exactly like a smaller version of the TU-104. The second production batch, designated TU-124V, became
the standard, and has an increased seating capacity of
56.

TUPOLEV TU-134

Country of Origin: Soviet Union

Production: Number built 720 plus; in airline service 651 plus

Power Plant: Two 6,800kgp (14,490lb st) Soloviev D-30 turbofans

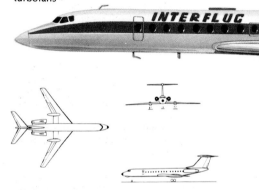

Performance: Max cruising speed 900km/h (559mph) at 8,500m (28,000ft); economical cruise 750km/h (466mph) at 11,000m (36,000ft); initial rate of climb 14.8m/sec (2,913ft/min); normal operating ceiling 12,000m (39,370ft); take-off field length 2,050m (6,726ft); range with 1hr reserve 2,400km (1,490mls) with 7,000kg (15,430lb) payload and 3,500km (2,175mls) with 3,000kg (6,600lb) payload

Weights: Operating weight empty 27,500kg (60,627lb); max payload 7,700kg (16,975lb); max fuel 13,000kg (28,660lb); max take-off 44,500kg (98,105lb); max landing 40,000kg (88,185lb); max zero-fuel 35,200kg (77,600lb)

Dimensions: Span 29.00m (95ft 3.75in); length 34.35m (112ft 8.25in); height 9.02m (29ft 7in); wing area 127.3sq m (1,370.3sq ft)

Seating Capacity: 72

History: Tested in prototype form in 1962 as the TU-124A, it eventually went into production in 1964 as the TU-134 and entered service with Aeroflot in September 1967 on the Moscow-Stockholm route. A stretched version, the TU-134A, seated up to 84 passengers. A subsequent version, the TU-134A3, is powered by the Soloviev D-30-111 turbofans, with accommodation for up to 96 passengers. The most recent version to enter service is the TU-134B, which features a revised cockpit for a three-man crew.

TUPOLEV TU-144

Country of Origin: Soviet Union
Production: Number built 13
Power Plant: Four 20,000kgp (44,000lb st) with reheat Kuznetsov NK-44 turbofans

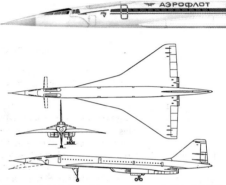

Performance: Max cruising speed up to Mach 2.35 (2,500mk/h/1,550mph) at altitudes of up to 18,000m (59,000ft); normal cruise Mach 2.2 (2,300km/h/1,430mph); max range with full payload 6,500km (4,030mls) at an average Mach 1.9 (2,000km/h/1,243mph)
Weights: Operating weight empty 85,000kg (187,400lb); max payload 14,000kg (30,865lb); max fuel load 95,000kg (209,440lb); max take-off weight

180,000kg (396,830lb); max landing weight 120,000kg (264,550lb)

Dimensions: Span 28.80m (94ft 6in); length 65.70m (215ft 6.5in); height 12.85m (42ft 2in); wing area 438sq m (4,714.5sq ft)

Seating Capacity: 140

History: The world's first supersonic airliner to fly, the SST TU-144 resembles Concorde very closely, being only marginally larger and faster. First prototype flight was on 3 December 1968, with the first supersonic flight on 5 June 1969 with Mach 2 first achieved on 26 May 1970. At the 1973 Paris Air Show the first production model appeared, having undergone considerable alteration in the years since its first prototype flight: it was larger overall, with uprated relocated engines and new wings with straight leading edges. The TU-144 entered service with Aeroflot on 26 December 1975 on the Moscow-Alma Ata route, but services were halted on 1 June 1978 immediately following an accident to one of the airliners, and have not been resumed.

TUPOLEV TU-154

Country of Origin: Soviet Union
Production: Number built 630 plus; in airline service
575 plus
Power Plant: Three 9,500kgp (20,950lb st) Kuznetsov
NK-8-2 turbofans

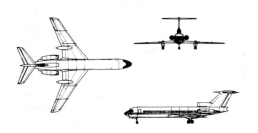

Performance: Max cruising speed 975km/h (605mph)
at 9,500m (31,150ft); best-cost cruise 900km/h
(560mph); long-range cruise 850km/h (528mph); bal-
anced take-off distance 2,100m (6,890ft); landing field
length 2,060m (6,758ft); range with max payload and
1hr reserve 3,460km (2,150mls); range with max fuel

and 13,650kg (30,100lb) payload, 5,280km (3,280mls)

Weights: Operating weight empty 43,500kg (95,900lb); max payload 20,000kg (44,090lb); max fuel load 33,150kg (73,085lb); max take-off weight 90,000kg (198,416lb); max landing weight 80,000kg (176,370lb); max zero fuel weight 63,633kg (139,994lb)

Dimensions: Span 37.55m (123ft 2.5in); length 47.90m (157ft 1.75in); wing area 201.45sq m (2,169sq ft)

Seating Capacity: 128

History: First flown on 4 October 1968, first deliveries reached Aeroflot in 1971, although it did not enter full passenger service until 9 February 1972. The first internal route was Moscow-Mineralnye Vady, and international operation began on 1 August 1972 between Moscow and Prague. The TU-154A entered service in 1975 (having first flown in 1973), with up-rated NK-8-2U engines. In 1977 the TU-154B appeared; it was capable of accommodating 169 passengers in single-class layout.

YAKOVLEV YAK-40

Country of Origin: Soviet Union
Production: Number built 1,000 plus; in airline service 803 plus
Power Plant: Three 1,500kgp (3,300lb st) Ivchenko A1-25 turbofans

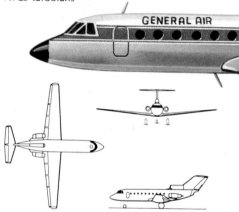

Performance: Max cruising speed 600km/h (373mph) at sea level; max cruising speed 550km/h (324mph) at 6,000m (19,685ft); initial rate of climb 8.0m/sec (1,575ft.min); typical take-off run 600m (1,968ft); typical landing roll 500m (1,804ft); range with max fuel, 45min reserve, 950km (590mls) at max cruise speed;

max range, no reserves, 1,450km (900mls) at 420km/h (261mph) at 8,000m (26,247ft)

Weights: Empty 9,135kg (20,140lb); max payload 2,300kg (5,070lb); max take-off and landing weight 14,700kg (32,410lb)

Dimensions: Span 25.0m (82ft 0.25in); length 20.36m (66ft 9.5in); height 6.50m (21ft4in); wing area 70.0sq m (753.5sq ft)

Seating Capacity: 27

History: The first cruise aircraft to be designed by the Yakovlev design bureau, the YAK-40 first flew on 21 October 1966. Production commenced the following year, with first deliveries being made to Aeroflot in 1968. The YAK-40V has been successfully exported to Italy, Germany, Afghanistan and Czechoslovakia, but the proposed stretched variant, the YAK-40M, never materialized.

YAKOVLEV YAK-42

Country of Origin: Soviet Union

Production: Number built 60 plus; in airline service 60 plus

Power Plant: Three Lotarev D-36 high by-pass turbofans each rated at 6,440kgp (14,200lb st)

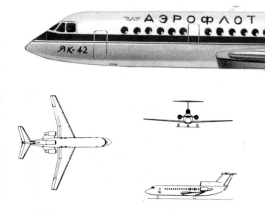

Performance: Normal cruising speed 820km/h (510mph); high speed cruise 870km/h (540mph); range 1,850km (1,150mls) with 12,000kg (26,430lb) payload; airfield requirement 1,800m (5,900ft)

Weights: Max take-off 52,000kg (114,535lb); max

payload 14,500kg (31,940lb)

Dimensions: Span 34.20m (112ft 2.5in); length 36.38m (119ft 4in); height 9.83m (32ft 3in); wing area 150sq m (1,614.6sq ft)

Seating Capacity: 120

History: The YAK-42 was designed as a fuel efficient replacement for the TU-134 and Il-18 on short-range trunk routes and possibly the An-24 on internal Aeroflot routes but with a reduced seating capacity of 100. First flown on 7 March 1973, the aircraft entered service in 1980 with some 60 aircraft being built. These were withdrawn from service in 1982, returning 2 years later after possibly undergoing essential modifications. During that time production was halted, and is expected to resume in 1987 but on a stretched version, the YAK-42M, some 4.5m (14ft 9in) longer, with seating capacity of 156-168.

Index

238